RAINBOW LORIKEETS live in Australia, New Guinea, Indonesia, and some Pacific Islands.

BEHAVIOR Rainbow lorikeets break up into smaller flocks to find food; these flocks usually have only about 20 birds.

CHARACTERISTIC The rainbow lorikeet has feet with two toes pointing forward and two toes pointing backward.

BEHAVIOR Rainbow lorikeets make a lot of noise — they often screech and chatter.

HSP Pennsylvania Science

Harcourt
SCHOOL PUBLISHERS

Visit *The Learning Site!*
www.harcourtschool.com

HSP Pennsylvania Science

Harcourt
SCHOOL PUBLISHERS

ISBN – 13: 978-0-15-363764-3
ISBN – 10: 0-15-363764-1

3 4 5 6 7 8 9 10   0918   16 15 14 13 12 11 10

Excursion Photo Credits
Page Placement Key: (t) Top, (b) bottom, (l) left, (r) right, (c) center, (bg) background, (fg) foreground

Life: Life Strand Tab (bg) Mark Raycroft/Minden Pictures; 40 (b) G. Brad Lewis/Science Faction/Getty Images, (bg) Frans Lanting/Minden Pictures; 41 (b) age fotostock/SuperStock, (cr) Steven Lee Montgomery/Photo Resource Hawaii; 42 (b) David Lassman/Syracuse Newspapers/The Image Works, (cr) Long Acre Farms; 43 (bg) David Lassman/Syracuse Newspapers/The Image Works; 44 (b)(tl) Monte L. Bean Life Science Museum; 45 Monte L. Bean Life Science Museum.

Earth: Earth Strand Tab (bg) Scott T. Smith/Danita Delimont; 186 (br) Norbert Wu/Minden Pictures; (c) Thinkstock Images/JupiterImages; 187 (bg) G Brad Lewis/The Image Bank/Getty Images; 189 (b)(br) McConnell & McNamara; (bg) Paul Rezendes/AGPix; 190 (bg) Ray Ng/Time Life Pictures/Getty Images; (cr) Stephen Saks Photography/Alamy; 191 (cl) Tom Tracy Photography/Alamy; (tl) NASA Jet Propulsion Laboratory.

Physical: Physical Strand Tab (bg) Macduff Everton/The Image Works; 348 (bg) ThinkStock/SuperStock; 349 (tl) G. Brad Lewis/Science Faction/Getty Images; (cl) Macduff Everton/The Image Bank/Getty Images; (br) Royalty-Free/Corbis; 350 (bc) McConnell & McNamara; (bg) Enigma/Alamy; 351 (tl) Comstock/SuperStock; 352 (br) Mike Quinn/National Park Service 353 (bg) Dmitri Bogdanov Photography/photographersdirect.com.

Consulting Authors

Michael J. Bell
*Associate Professor of Early
Childhood Education*
College of Education
West Chester University of
Pennsylvania
West Chester, Pennsylvania

Michael A. DiSpezio
Curriculum Architect
JASON Academy
Cape Cod, Massachusetts

Marjorie Frank
*Former Adjunct Professor, Science
Education*
Hunter College
New York, New York

Gerald H. Krockover
*Professor of Earth and Atmospheric
Science Education*
Purdue University
West Lafayette, Indiana

Joyce C. McLeod
Adjunct Professor
Rollins College
Winter Park, Florida

Barbara ten Brink
Science Specialist
Austin Independent School
District
Austin, Texas

Carol J. Valenta
Senior Vice President
St. Louis Science Center
St. Louis, Missouri

Barry A. Van Deman
President and CEO
Museum of Life and Science
Durham, North Carolina

Senior Editorial Advisors

Napoleon Adebola Bryant, Jr.
Professor Emeritus of Education
Xavier University
Cincinnati, Ohio

Tyrone Howard
Associate Professor
Graduate School of Education and
Information Studies
University of California, Los Angeles
Los Angeles, California

Robert M. Jones
Professor of Education Foundations
University of Houston–Clear Lake
Houston, Texas

Mozell P. Lang
Former Science Consultant
Michigan Department of Education
Science Consultant, Highland Park
Schools
Highland Park, Michigan

Jerry D. Valadez
K–12 Science Coordinator
Fresno Unified School District
Fresno, California

Contents

Big Idea
People learn about science by asking good questions and doing careful investigations.

LIFE SCIENCE

A — A World of Living Things — 47

Big Idea
Living things have needs and change as they grow.

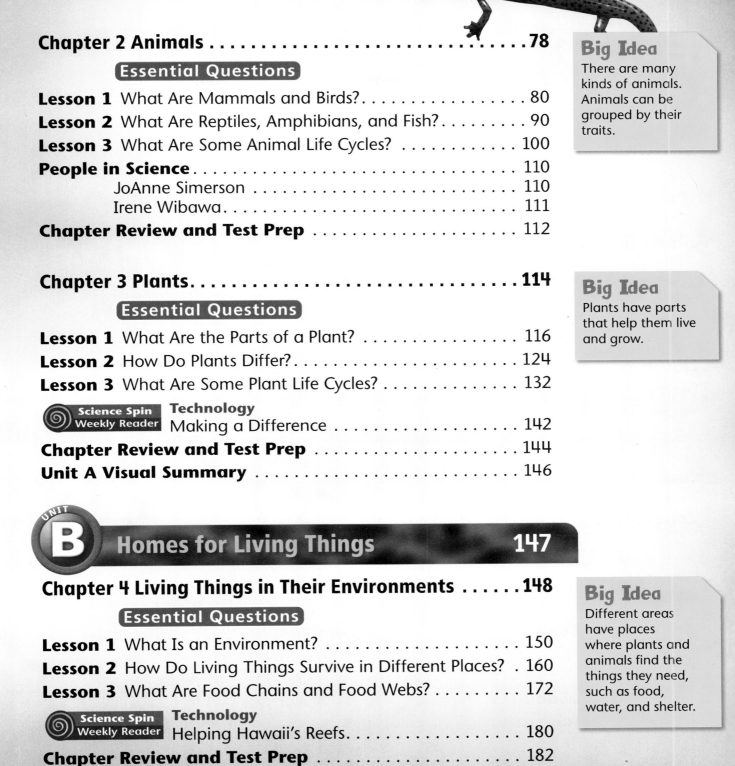

Big Idea
There are many kinds of animals. Animals can be grouped by their traits.

Big Idea
Plants have parts that help them live and grow.

UNIT B Homes for Living Things 147

Big Idea
Different areas have places where plants and animals find the things they need, such as food, water, and shelter.

v

EARTH SCIENCE

UNIT C Our Earth   193

Big Idea
Earth's surface is made up of many different materials and can change over time.

Big Idea
Earth has many natural resources that people use. It is important to protect them to make them last.

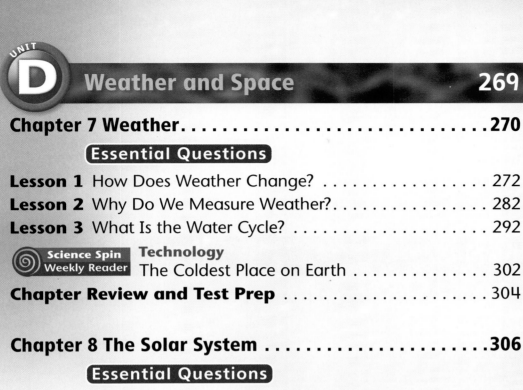

UNIT D Weather and Space 269

Big Idea
Weather can be observed, measured, predicted, and compared.

Big Idea
Earth is a planet. Changes happen on Earth and in the sky from day to night and from season to season.

PHYSICAL SCIENCE

UNIT E   Exploring Matter   355

Big Idea
There are three states of matter: solid, liquid, and gas.

Big Idea
Matter can change.

F UNIT

Energy in Motion

Big Idea
Light and heat are forms of energy.

Big Idea
Sound can travel and is caused by vibrations.

Big Idea
We can observe and measure the ways things move.

REFERENCES

Ready, Set, Science!

What's the Big Idea?

People learn about science by asking good questions and doing careful investigations.

Essential Questions

Student eBook
www.hspscience.com

x

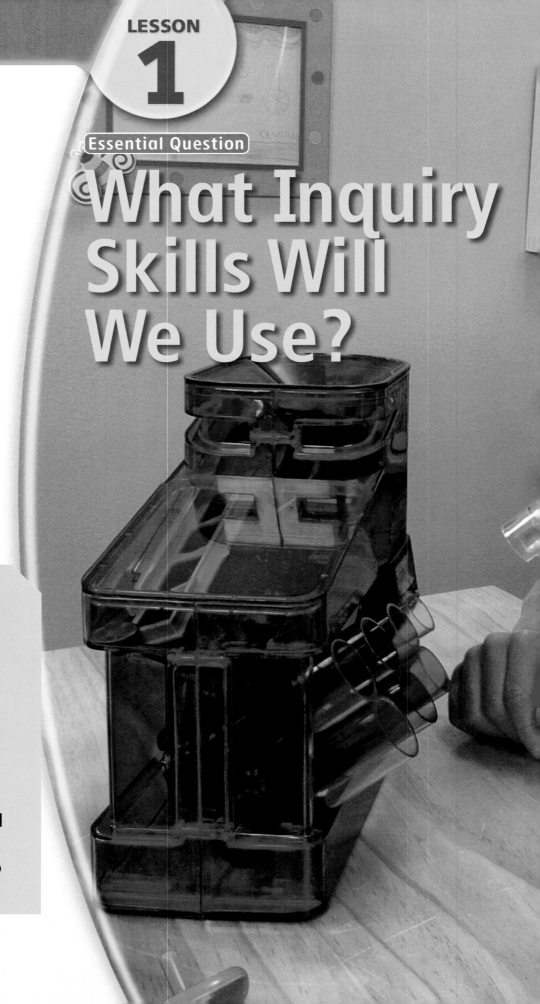

Investigate to find how many pennies will fit into a plastic jar.

Read and Learn about science inquiry skills.

Essential Question

What Inquiry Skills Will We Use?

Fast Fact

Observing Objects

A penny is like a sandwich made of metal. The inside layer is made of a metal called zinc. The outside layers are made of a metal called copper. You can observe coins to learn about them.

Inquiry skills are a set of skills people use to find out information. (p. 6)

girl sorting coins

How Many Pennies?

Ask a Question

These children have found some coins. What can they observe about the coins? Investigate to find out. Then read and learn to find out more.

Get Ready

Inquiry Skill Tip
When you observe, you use your senses, such as sight and touch, to find out more about an object.

You need

pennies

plastic jar or cup

4

What to Do

Step ①

Observe some pennies and a jar. Predict and write the number of pennies that you think will fill the jar.

Step ②

Fill the jar with pennies. Count and write the number of pennies that fit.

Step ③

Compare the number of pennies in the jar with the number you predicted.

Draw Conclusions

Was your prediction correct?

Independent Inquiry

When you **observe**, you can use your senses of sight and touch. Observe how many dimes fill the same jar you used for the Investigate.

VOCABULARY
inquiry skills

 **MAIN IDEA AND DETAILS**

Look for details about the inquiry skills that scientists use.

Inquiry Skills

Scientists use inquiry skills when they do tests. **Inquiry skills** help people find out information.

Observe

Use your five senses to observe. Learn about things around you.

Compare

Observe ways things are alike and ways they are different.

Classify

Classify things by comparing them and sorting them into groups to show ways they are alike.

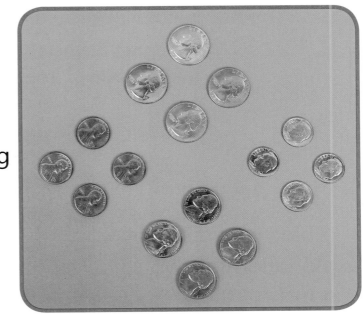

Make a Model

Make a model to show what something is like or how it works.

Focus Skill **MAIN IDEA AND DETAILS**

What are some inquiry skills?

A magnet attracts things made of iron.

Hypothesize

Think of a scientific explanation that you can test.

The ball went really far! I must have thrown it hard.

Infer

Use what you know to make a good guess about what is happening.

Draw Conclusions

Use the information you have gathered to decide whether your conclusion is correct.

⭐ **MAIN IDEA AND DETAILS**

Why are inferring and drawing conclusions inquiry skills?

I think this plant needs water.

sequence of size

sequence of value

Sequence

Put things in order to show changes.

Measure

Use tools to find out how much. You can measure how long, wide, or tall something is. You can measure how much something weighs. You can measure how much space something takes up.

I think it's going to rain.

Predict

Use what you know to make a good guess about what will happen.

 MAIN IDEA AND DETAILS
What are some ways you can measure?

Stacking Pennies

Set a tray on a table. Predict what will happen if you try to stack 50 pennies. Stack the pennies. What happens? Was your prediction correct?

11

Plan an Investigation

Figure out what you will do to find out what you want to know.

Record and Communicate

Record information by drawing or writing about it. Share what you know by showing or telling others.

Focus Skill MAIN IDEA AND DETAILS

Why is communicating an inquiry skill?

What inquiry skills will we use?

In this lesson, you learned about inquiry skills. You also learned how to use them to find out more about what you want to know.

1. **MAIN IDEA AND DETAILS**
Make a chart like this one. Fill in details about this main idea. **Inquiry skills help people find out information.**

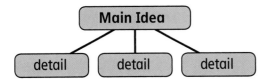

2. VOCABULARY Use the term **inquiry skills** to tell about this picture.

3. DRAW CONCLUSIONS What inquiry skills would you use to find out more about a pinecone?

4. SUMMARIZE Write two sentences that tell what the lesson is about.

Test Prep

5. What should you do if you want to find out how wide a box is?

Make Connections

Writing

Sentences to Compare
Observe a penny and a nickel. Write a few sentences. Tell ways the penny and the nickel are alike and ways they are different.

13

What Science Tools Will We Use?

Investigate to find out how many drops of water will fit on a penny.

Read and Learn about science tools.

Fast Fact

Ways To Measure

If you want to measure an object and you do not have a ruler or a tape measure, you can use your hand to see how many hands long the object is. You can predict a measurement and then measure to see if the prediction is correct.

14

People use **science tools** to find information. (p. 18)

The Nature of **Heat**

Radiation　　Conduction

Heat on Matter

Gas

School is cool.

Respect your enviro

Drops of Water on a Penny

Guided Inquiry

Ask a Question

This boy just flipped a coin. Now the children are observing. What are they predicting?
Investigate to find out. Then read and learn to find out more.

Get Ready

Inquiry Skill Tip

When you predict, you tell what you think might happen.

You need

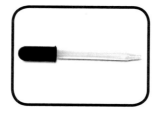

dropper

cup of water

coin

16

What to Do

Step ①

Predict the number of water drops you can put on a coin before the water runs off. Write your **prediction**.

Step ②

Use the dropper to drop water on the coin. Count the drops. Stop when the water starts to run off the coin.

Step ③

Compare your **prediction** with the number of drops you were able to put on the coin.

Draw Conclusions

Was your prediction correct? If you do the Investigate again, will you get the same answer?

Independent Inquiry

When you **predict**, you tell what you think will happen. Predict how many drops of liquid soap you can fit on the same coin.

VOCABULARY
science tools

MAIN IDEA AND DETAILS
Look for details about science tools.

Science Tools

When scientists want to find out about things, they use different tools. These **science tools** are used to help people find out information.

Hand Lens

Use a hand lens to magnify objects, or make them look larger. Hold the hand lens near your face. Move the object until you can see it clearly.

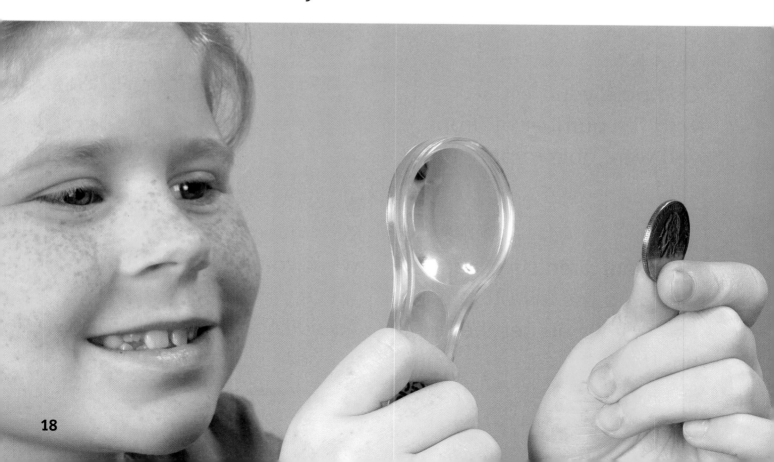

18

Magnifying Box

Use a magnifying box to make an object look larger. Place the object in the box. Then look through the top of the box.

Forceps

Use forceps to hold or move small objects so you can see them better or separate them.

 MAIN IDEA AND DETAILS

What are some objects you might want to use a hand lens to observe?

Observe a Coin

Use a hand lens to look at a coin. Then use a magnifying box to look at it. Draw what you observe.

Ruler

Use a ruler to measure how long, wide, or tall an object is. Put the first mark of the ruler at one end of the object. Read the number at the other end of the object.

Tape Measure

Use a tape measure to measure length, width, and height. Use a tape measure to measure around an object. Many rulers and tape measures use centimeters as the unit of measurement.

Measuring Cup

Use a measuring cup to measure a liquid. Liquids can be measured in units called liters and milliliters.

Place the cup on a table. Pour the liquid into the cup. When the liquid stops moving, read the mark at the top of the liquid.

(Focus Skill) MAIN IDEA AND DETAILS

Why is a measuring cup a useful science tool?

Balance

Use a balance to measure the mass of an object. Mass is measured in grams and kilograms.

Place the object on one side of the balance. Place masses on the other side. Add or remove masses until the two sides of the balance are even.

Add the masses to find the mass of the object.

Scale

Use a scale to measure the weight of an object. Weight is measured in units called pounds and ounces.

Make sure the scale is at zero. Then place the object you want to weigh on the scale. Read the number.

Thermometer

Use a thermometer to measure temperature. Temperature is measured in units called degrees. Some thermometers show both Celsius and Fahrenheit degrees.

Place the thermometer where you want to measure the temperature. On the thermometer, read the number next to the top of the liquid.

 **MAIN IDEA AND DETAILS**

Why is a thermometer a science tool?

Fahrenheit   Celsius

Dropper

Use a dropper to place small amounts of a liquid. Squeeze the bulb of the dropper. Then put the dropper in the liquid and slowly stop squeezing. To drop the liquid, slowly squeeze the bulb again.

lens

slide

Simple Microscope

Use a microscope to make very tiny objects look larger. Put the objects on the slide, and look at the slide through the lens.

Focus Skill **MAIN IDEA AND DETAILS**

Which of these tools helps you observe small objects?

Essential Question

What science tools will we use?

In this lesson, you learned about tools that scientists use to find out more about things.

1. ⭐ **MAIN IDEA AND DETAILS**
Make a chart like this one. Fill in details about this main idea. **Scientists use tools.**

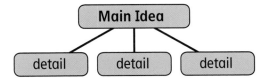

```
          Main Idea
      /       |       \
  detail   detail   detail
```

2. VOCABULARY Use the term **science tools** to tell how to observe an insect.

3. DRAW CONCLUSIONS How are a ruler and a tape measure alike? How are they different?

4. SUMMARIZE Write two sentences that tell what this lesson is mostly about. Use the term **science tool**.

Test Prep

5. Which tool would you use to look at something very small?

A a hand lens
B a measuring cup
C a ruler
D a thermometer

Make Connections

 **Math**

Estimate and Count

Estimate the number of pennies you need to make a row as long as a ruler. Then lay pennies beside a ruler. Count the pennies. How many do you need? Is the number of pennies more than, less than, or the same as your estimate?

Investigate to find out how to compare coins.

Read and Learn about scientists and how they work.

Essential Question

How Do Scientists Work?

Fast Fact

Investigating Objects

For thousands of years, scientists have been investigating and sharing their conclusions. You, too, can do investigations. You can compare objects to see how they are alike and different.

To **investigate** is to plan and do a test. Scientists investigate to answer a question. (p. 30)

Equal Coins

Ask a Question

This coin has many details. What are some ways this child can find out more about the coin? Investigate to find out. Then read and learn to find out more.

Get Ready

You need

quarter

5 nickels

balance

What to Do

Step ①

A quarter and 5 nickels both equal 25 cents. Does a quarter have the same mass as 5 nickels? **Compare** to find out.

Step ②

Make sure the balance is even. Then place the quarter on one side of the balance and the 5 nickels on the other side.

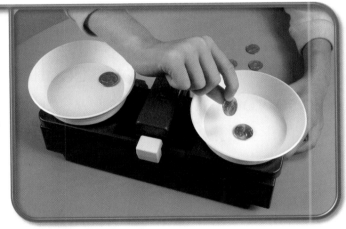

Step ③

Compare the two sides of the balance.

Draw Conclusions

Are the two sides of the balance even? Why do you think that is?

Independent Inquiry

When you **compare**, you observe ways things are alike and different. Compare the mass of two dimes and a nickel with a quarter.

VOCABULARY

investigate

SEQUENCE

Look for the order of the steps scientists use when they are investigating.

Investigating

When scientists want to answer a question or solve a problem, they **investigate**, or plan and do a test. Your teacher may give instructions for doing an investigation. You need to follow these instructions carefully. Or you may do your own investigation. When you investigate, you use a plan like this.

1. Observe, and ask a question.

Think of a question you want to answer. Write what you already know about the topic of your question. Figure out what information you need.

Does the mass of a real quarter equal the mass of a play quarter?

The mass of a real quarter is greater than the mass of a play quarter. This is because they are made of different things.

2. Form a hypothesis.

Write a hypothesis, or a scientific explanation that you can test.

3. Plan a fair test.

A fair test will help you answer your question. List things you will need and steps you will follow to do the test. Decide what you want to learn from the test.

(Focus Skill) **SEQUENCE** What should you do after you form a hypothesis?

Insta-Lab

Wet Quarters

Wet a quarter. Place the quarter on the mouth of a glass bottle. Wrap your hands around the neck of the bottle. What do you observe?

4. Do the test.

Follow the steps of your plan. Observe carefully. Record everything that happens. Repeat your test. You should get the same answers.

5. Draw conclusions, and communicate results.

Think about what you found out. Was your hypothesis correct? Use what you found out to draw conclusions. Then communicate your results with others.

My hypothesis was correct!

Focus Skill SEQUENCE What should you do before you draw conclusions?

Investigate more.

If your hypothesis was correct, ask another question about your topic to test. If your hypothesis was not correct, form another hypothesis and change the test.

Focus Skill SEQUENCE What should you do if your hypothesis was correct?

Will a real dime have the same mass as a play dime?

How do scientists work?

In this lesson, you learned ways scientists think and how they work to answer questions.

1. ⭐ **SEQUENCE**
Make a chart like this one. Show the steps scientists use to investigate.

2. VOCABULARY Use the term **investigate** to tell about this lesson.

3. DRAW CONCLUSIONS If you had a question about something, how could you find the answer?

4. SUMMARIZE Write two sentences that tell what the lesson is about.

Test Prep

5. What is a hypothesis?

Make Connections

 Art

Coin Rubbings

Place coins under a sheet of paper. Use crayons of different colors to make rubbings of the coins. Label each coin with its name. Why can you make rubbings of coins?

Vocabulary Review

Use the terms to complete the sentences. The page numbers tell you where to look if you need help.

inquiry skills p. 6   **investigate** p. 30

science tools p. 18

1. Comparing and measuring are two _____.

2. If you want to find out something, you can _____.

3. Scientists use _____ to find out information.

Check Understanding

4. Which one of the following details
   (Focus Skill) is correct?

   A A hand lens is an inquiry skill.
   B Classifying is an inquiry skill.
   C A dropper is an inquiry skill.
   D A coin is an inquiry skill.

5. What is the next step you should do after you ask a question?

    F Investigate more.

    G Draw conclusions.

    H Plan a fair test.

    J Form a hypothesis.

Critical Thinking

6. Look at the picture.

Why are the things on the table science tools?

7. Why must Miguel do a fair test if he wants to find out information?

The

Safety in Science

Here are some safety rules to follow when you do activities.

1. **Think ahead.** Study the steps and follow them.

2. **Be neat and clean.** Wipe up spills right away.

3. **Watch your eyes.** Wear safety goggles when told to do so.

4. **Be careful with sharp things.**

5. **Do not eat or drink things.**

LIFE SCIENCE

PENNSYLVANIA

Prospect

Big BUTLER Fair

People come to this big fair from all over. Farmers come to show the animals they raise and the crops they grow. People come to the fair to see these things and to have fun. Children like to ride the fair rides. Many people like to listen to music at the fair.

Children at the Fair

Many children wait all year for the fair. They raise and take care of animals themselves to show at the fair. They might raise pigs, cows, or sheep. At the fair, judges look at the animals. They choose the best ones. The children who raised these animals win ribbons.

Farmers at the Fair

At the fair, you can see many things farmers grow in our state. Some raise cows and pigs. Others may grow plants for food. They grow wheat and corn. We eat parts of the wheat and corn plants. Wheat and corn are used to make bread, cakes, and cereal.

sheep grazing

chicks

Think And Write

1 **Scientific Thinking** What plants are grown near you? Why do those plants grow well?

2 **Scientific Thinking** What do you think a sheep's coat can be used for?

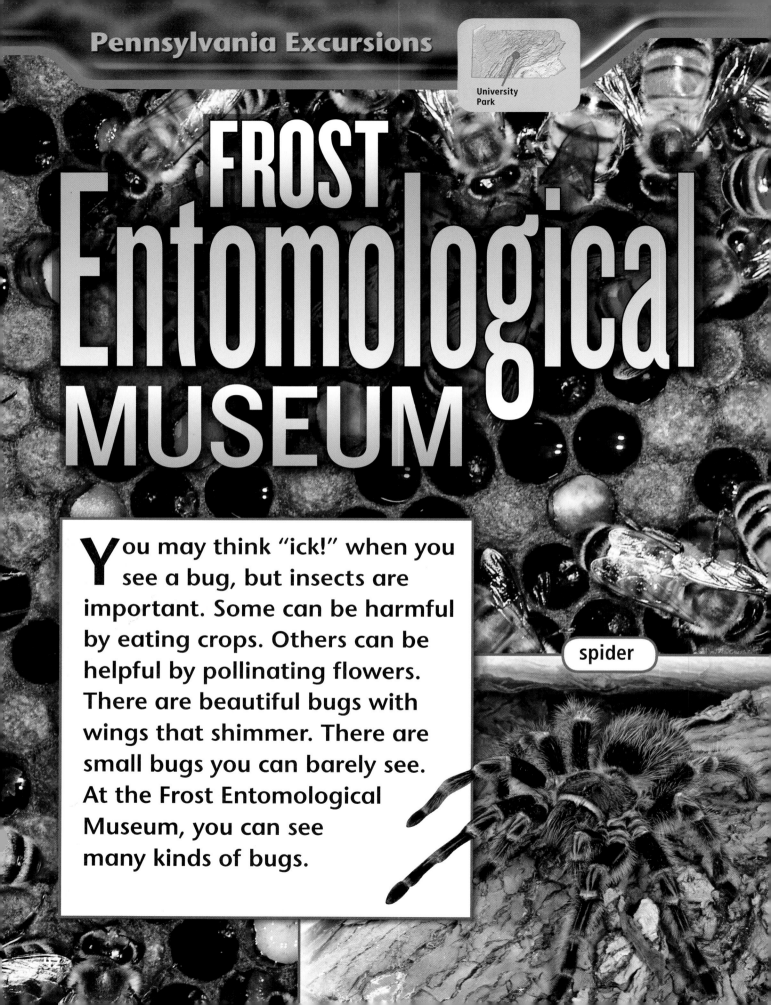

University Park

FROST Entomological MUSEUM

You may think "ick!" when you see a bug, but insects are important. Some can be harmful by eating crops. Others can be helpful by pollinating flowers. There are beautiful bugs with wings that shimmer. There are small bugs you can barely see. At the Frost Entomological Museum, you can see many kinds of bugs.

spider

Bugs Up Close

At the museum, you can find out about bugs. You can find out what bugs live in our state. You can learn why bugs are important in our world. There are some live bugs you can watch crawl around. You can even find out how bugs help police solve crimes!

Special Stuff About Bugs

If you really like bugs, you might want to go to Bug Camp for Kids. You can do that at the center. There is also a Great Insect Fair at the center every summer. At the fair, you can watch insect races. You can see many kinds of live insects. You can even eat something insects make— honey!

Think And Write

1 **Scientific Thinking** How do bugs both help and harm crops?

2 **Scientific Thinking** Think of insects that bite or sting you. What are some ways you can keep this from happening?

giant hissing cockroach

Fall Photography *in* Pennsylvania

Fall in our state is beautiful to see. As the weather gets colder, leaves on the trees change color. Some leaves turn yellow, orange, or red. People come from all over to see fall in our state. They travel the roads in their cars. They stop to look at the beautiful leaves across the mountains. Fall is a thrilling sight!

Saving Memories of Fall

Many people who visit our state in fall take photographs. Some put their photographs in books. Others make them bigger. They put these photo posters on their walls like art. Then they can have the colors of fall all the time.

Taking Pictures

People use different kinds of cameras, some with film and some without. No matter what camera you use, you should plan your picture. You might see one tree covered with red leaves. That could be the center of the picture. Behind that tree might be many trees of another color. Be sure not to move the camera while you are taking the picture, or it may turn out blurry.

Think And Write

1. **Scientific Thinking** Why do leaves change color in fall?

2. **Scientific Thinking** Why are photographs a good way to remember fall?

Project — A Habitat Diorama

Materials
- shoe box
- scissors
- tape or glue
- old magazines
- construction paper
- string

Procedure
1. Choose an animal from our state. One animal might be a ruffed grouse.
2. Find pictures of the animal. Cut out the pictures. (Ask an adult before you begin.)
3. List what the animal needs to live. For example, a grouse needs water to drink.
4. Make a diorama of the animal and its habitat. Show what the animal needs to live. Show its shelter, what it eats, and what it drinks. If your diorama shows the animal smaller than it is, everything in the box should be smaller, too.

Draw Conclusions
1. You made a list of what animals need to live. How might your knowing that help save animals in the wild?
2. You made a model. How does that help you know what the animal needs?

A World of Living Things

UNIT A — **LIFE SCIENCE**

Unit Inquiry

Plants and Light
As you do this unit, you will learn what living things need. Plan and do a test. Find out how light changes the growth of plants.

CHAPTER 1

Living and Nonliving Things

Living things have needs and change as they grow.

Essential Questions

Lesson 1

What Are Living and Nonliving Things?

Lesson 2

What Do Animals Need?

Lesson 3

What Do Plants Need?

Student eBook
www.hspscience.com

deer drinking from a stream

Things can be living, nonliving, or once-living. Is this deer living or nonliving? How do you know? Think about the **Big Idea** to help you answer.

Essential Question

What Are Living and Nonliving Things?

Investigate to find out how to classify living and nonliving things.

Read and Learn about living and nonliving things.

Fast Fact

Alike and Different

A live frog has a sticky tongue that helps it get food. A model of a frog, such as a garden statue, is not alive, so it does not need food. You can classify things to see how they are alike and different.

frog on a frog statue

A **living** thing is alive. Plants and animals are living things because they need food, water, and oxygen. (p. 54)

Oxygen is a gas that is in air and water. Most living things need oxygen. (p. 54)

A **nonliving** thing is not alive. Air, water, and rocks are nonliving. (p. 56)

51

Living or Nonliving

Ask a Question

Living things have needs. What things in this picture are living? Investigate to find out. Then read and learn to find out more.

Get Ready

Inquiry Skill Tip

When you classify things, you group them by how they are alike and how they are different. You can make a chart to show how you classify things.

You need

paper and pencil

What to Do

Step ①

Go outside with your class. Draw pictures to record some of the things you see.

Step ②

Classify your pictures. Make a chart like this one.

Living and Nonliving	
Living	Nonliving

Step ③

Use the chart to talk about what you saw.

Draw Conclusions

Which things are living? Which things are not living?

Independent Inquiry

Classifying things helps you see how they are alike or different. Classify living things by whether they are plants or animals.

VOCABULARY
living
oxygen
nonliving

COMPARE AND CONTRAST
Look for ways living and nonliving things are alike and different.

Living Things

Living things need food, water, and **oxygen**, a gas in air and in water. Living things grow and change. They can also make new living things like themselves.

All animals are living things. Animals need food, water, and oxygen. Over time, animals grow bigger and change. Adult animals can make new animals.

Plants are also living things. Like animals, they need food and water. They also need oxygen and other gases. Plants grow and change. They can make new plants.

You can see living things everywhere on Earth. What living things are in this picture?

 **COMPARE AND CONTRAST** How are animals and plants alike?

What Living Things Need

Draw a picture of a plant or an animal. Then list the things it needs that show it is a living thing. Share your list with a classmate.

Nonliving Things

Nonliving things do not need food, water, and oxygen. They cannot make new things like themselves. Water, air, and rocks are nonliving things.

Focus Skill COMPARE AND CONTRAST What living and nonliving things are in the picture below? How are they different?

What are living and nonliving things?

In this lesson, you learned that living things have needs and grow and that nonliving things do not have needs and do not grow.

1.  **COMPARE AND CONTRAST** Make a chart like this one. Tell how living and nonliving things are alike and how they are different.

alike	different

2. VOCABULARY Explain the meanings of the terms **living** and **nonliving**.

3. DRAW CONCLUSIONS If something does not need food or water, is it **living** or **nonliving**?

4. SUMMARIZE Use the chart to write a lesson summary.

Test Prep

5. If something needs water, what must it be?
  A an animal
  B a living thing
  C a nonliving thing
  D a plant

Make Connections

 Writing

Description of How I Am Changing
You are a living thing. Draw a picture that shows how you looked as a baby and how you look today. Write sentences that tell how you have grown and changed.

I'm taller and I have more teeth.

Investigate to find out how to observe what animals need.

Read and Learn about animal needs.

Essential Question

What Do Animals Need?

Fast Fact

Observing Birds
Birds build nests that hold their eggs and keep their chicks safe. You can find out what animals need by observing them.

bird leaving its nest

To **survive** is to stay alive. Animals need food and water to survive. (p. 62)

Shelter is a safe place to live. Birds may use a nest for shelter. (p. 63)

59

What Birds Eat

Ask a Question

This hummingbird has needs. How is it filling its needs in this picture?

Investigate to find out. Then read and learn to find out more.

Get Ready

Inquiry Skill Tip

When you observe things, you watch closely to see what happens. You can make a chart to show what you observed.

You need

dish of birdseed

dish of berries

dish of bread crumbs

What to Do

Step ①
With your teacher, place three kinds of bird food outside where birds can find them.

Step ②
Observe the bird food in the morning, at noon, and in the afternoon. Record your **observations** in a chart.

What Birds Eat

	birdseed	berries	bread crumbs
morning			
noon			
afternoon			

Step ③
Use your chart to tell what you **observed** about what birds outside your school like to eat.

Draw Conclusions
At what time of day did the birds you observed eat the most?

Independent Inquiry

When you **observe** animals, you can learn more about their needs. Make observations about how birds use food and water.

VOCABULARY
survive
shelter

MAIN IDEA AND DETAILS

Look for details about the things animals need to live.

Food and Water

Animals need food and water to **survive**, or stay alive. Bigger animals need more food than smaller ones. Whales and bears need more food than rabbits and owls.

As an animal grows, it needs more food and water. An adult bird needs more food than a young bird.

MAIN IDEA AND DETAILS What do animals need to survive?

bird with a fish

prairie dogs

bear in a cave

Space and Shelter

Animals need space. They need room to move around, find food, and care for their young.

Animals also need shelter. **Shelter** is a safe place to live. Prairie dogs dig holes for shelter. There they hide from animals that could eat them. The holes also keep them safe from bad weather. Owls and squirrels use trees for shelter. Some tigers and bears use caves.

MAIN IDEA AND DETAILS

Why do animals need space?

Clay Nest

Make a nest out of clay. How does a nest help keep eggs and chicks safe?

How Fish Get Oxygen

All animals need oxygen, but they get it in different ways. People and many animals use lungs to get oxygen from air. Fish use gills to take in oxygen from water.

gills

For more links and animations, go to **www.hspscience.com**

64

Essential Question

What do animals need?

In this lesson, you learned that animals have needs, such as food, air, water, space, and shelter.

1. 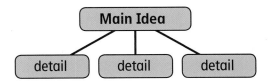 **MAIN IDEA AND DETAILS** Make a chart like this one. Fill in details about this main idea. **Animals need many things to survive.**

```
           Main Idea
        /      |      \
   detail   detail   detail
```

2. VOCABULARY Use the term **survive** to tell about this picture.

3. DRAW CONCLUSIONS Why do different kinds of animals need different kinds of shelter?

4. SUMMARIZE Write two sentences to tell what this lesson is mostly about. Start the first sentence with **Animals need.**

Test Prep

5. Why do most small animals need less food and water than larger animals?

Make Connections

 **Math**

Compare Amounts

Different animals need different amounts of food. Use the chart to compare how much food three dogs eat each day. Which eats the most? The least? How much would each dog eat in 3 days?

Number of Cups of Food

Dog	Day 1	Day 2	Day 3
Sandy	1	2	3
Rosey	2	4	6
Bo	3	6	9

Investigate to find out what plants need in order to grow.

Read and Learn about plant needs.

Essential Question

What Do Plants Need?

Fast Fact

Plant Needs

There are more than 300,000 kinds of plants. They all need the same things to live. Knowing the things all plants need helps you predict what will happen to plants that do not get them.

Nutrients are substances that plants and animals need to survive. Animals get nutrients from food. Plants get nutrients from the soil. (p. 70)

watering plants

What Plants Need to Grow

Guided Inquiry > **Ask a Question**

How can you tell these roses have what they need to grow? Investigate to find out. Then read and learn to find out more.

Get Ready

Inquiry Skill Tip

When you predict, you tell what you think will happen. Use what you have seen before to make your prediction.

You need

2 plants

cup of water

What to Do

Step ①

Put both plants in a sunny place. Water only one plant. **Predict** what will happen.

Step ②

Make a chart like this one.

Plant with water	Plant with no water

Step ③

Observe both plants every day. Water only one plant. Record any changes.

Draw Conclusions

Think about your prediction and what you observed. Was your **prediction** correct?

Independent Inquiry

When you **predict**, you use what you know to say what you think will happen. Predict what will happen to plants that get different amounts of light.

MAIN IDEA AND DETAILS

Look for details about what plants need to live.

Water, Light, and Air

Plants need water, light, and gases in air to live and grow. They also need **nutrients**, or substances that help them grow, from soil. Plants use all these things to make the food they need.

Different plants need different amounts of water. A cactus grows in a dry desert. A bald-cypress tree grows in a wet swamp. Big trees need much more water than tiny plants do.

Some plants need more light than others. Sunflowers need a lot of sun. Their stems get weak if they do not get enough light. Ferns need only a little sun. They can grow well in shade.

Focus Skill MAIN IDEA AND DETAILS

What do plants need to live?

Insta-Lab

Water in Soil

Put moist soil on a paper towel. Put another paper towel on top. Press down. Then remove the soil. What do you see on the paper towels? Wash your hands when you finish.

redwood trees

Room to Grow

As plants grow, they need more space. The roots and stems get bigger and longer. The plants have more leaves. A plant in a small container may need to be moved to a larger one to give it more room to grow.

Focus Skill) MAIN IDEA AND DETAILS

Why does a plant need room to grow?

Essential Question

What do plants need?

In this lesson, you learned that plants have needs, such as water, light, and air. Plants also need room to grow.

1. **Focus Skill** **MAIN IDEA AND DETAILS**
Make a chart like this one. Fill in details about this main idea. **Plants need many things to grow and stay healthy.**

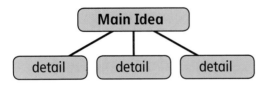

```
        Main Idea
       /    |    \
  detail  detail  detail
```

2. VOCABULARY
Why do plants need **nutrients**?

3. DRAW CONCLUSIONS What happens to a plant if it is not able to meet its needs?

4. SUMMARIZE Write two sentences that tell what this lesson is about.

Test Prep

5. What do all plants need?

   A water and no light

   B water and light

   C a lot of water

   D a lot of light

Make Connections

 Writing

Sweet Potato Journal
Stick toothpicks in a sweet potato to hold it partly in a jar of water. Put the jar in a sunny place. Observe the sweet potato for a month. Draw pictures and write sentences about how it changes.

Tomato Says, "Pass the Salt!"

According to experts, a large amount of U.S. farmland is too salty. They say each year about 101,000 square kilometers (38,000 square miles) of U.S. farmland cannot be used. The soil has too much salt.

Most plants can't grow in soil that has too much salt. But scientists have made a new kind of tomato that grows well in salty soil. The plant can even be watered with salty water.

A New Kind of Plant

Scientists have figured out a way to change how a tomato plant grows. The change allows the tomato plant to absorb salty water. The plant stores salt in its leaves, where it will not harm the plant or the fruit.

The scientists who grew the special tomatoes are also working on making other plants that can live in salty soil.

 Think and Write

How might plants that can grow in salty soil help farmers?

Salt of the Earth

Scientists say that plants such as corn, wheat, and peas could all be changed to be able to grow in salty soil.

Find out more. Log on to **www.hspscience.com**

Vocabulary Review

Use the terms below to complete the sentences. The page numbers tell you where to look if you need help.

living p. 54   **survive** p. 62

nonliving p. 56   **shelter** p. 63

1. A _____ thing does not need food, water, and air.

2. A cave may be a kind of _____.
3. Plants are _____ things.
4. Animals need food, water, and oxygen to _____.

Check Understanding

5. How are these things the same?

A They both need oxygen.
B They both need food.
C They are both living things.
D They are both nonliving things.

6. How are these animals alike?

F They both use gills to take in oxygen.

G They both use lungs to take in oxygen.

H They both need to take in oxygen.

J Neither of them needs to take in oxygen.

Critical Thinking

7. How are these plants different from nonliving things? The **Big Idea**

8. Think about what animals need to live. How will the needs of a rabbit change as it grows?

CHAPTER 2

Animals

What's the Big Idea?

There are many kinds of animals. Animals can be grouped by their traits.

Essential Questions

Lesson 1

What Are Mammals and Birds?

Lesson 2

What Are Reptiles, Amphibians, and Fish?

Lesson 3

What Are Some Animal Life Cycles?

GO online ▶ Student eBook
www.hspscience.com

What do YOU wonder?

These dolphins are mammals. How does this connect to the **Big Idea?**

Investigate to find out about hair and feathers.

Read and Learn about mammals and birds.

What Are Mammals and Birds?

Fast Fact

Animal Comparisons
No two zebras have exactly the same markings. You can compare animals in many ways.

A **mammal** is a member of the group of animals with hair or fur on their bodies.
(p. 84)

A **bird** is a member of the group of animals with feathers on their bodies and wings. Most birds can fly.
(p. 86)

zebra with birds

Compare Hair and Feathers

Guided Inquiry

Ask a Question

How do feathers help birds? Do any other kinds of animals have feathers?
Investigate to find out. Then read and learn to find out more.

Get Ready

Inquiry Skill Tip

When you compare things, you look for ways they are alike and ways they are different.

You need

feather

hand lens

What to Do

Step **①**

Observe the feather with the hand lens. What does it look like and feel like?

Step **②**

Observe the hair on your arm. **Compare** the hair with the feather.

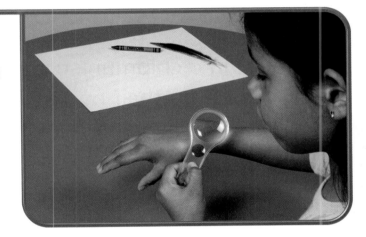

Step **③**

Draw pictures of what you observed.

Draw Conclusions

How are the feather and the hair alike and different? Write your answer.

Independent Inquiry

Comparing helps you understand how things are alike and different. How are birds and mammals alike and different?

VOCABULARY
mammal
bird

 **COMPARE AND CONTRAST**
Look for ways mammals and birds are alike and different.

Mammals

Scientists look at animals' body parts when they group animals. A **mammal** has fur or hair that covers the skin on its body. Most mammal mothers give birth to live young. The young drink milk from their mothers' bodies.

A lion and a chipmunk are mammals. They have fur on their bodies. Their young are born live and drink milk from their mothers' bodies.

chipmunk

lion and cub

manatees

dolphin

A manatee is also a mammal. A manatee does not have fur. But it does have some hair on its skin. A manatee mother gives birth to live young. The young drink milk from their mother's body. A manatee lives in water, but it has lungs, like other mammals. A manatee must rise to the top of the water to breathe in oxygen from the air.

A dolphin is a mammal, too. A dolphin mother gives birth to live young. The young drink milk from their mother's body. A dolphin uses its lungs to breathe in oxygen from the air.

Focus Skill COMPARE AND CONTRAST

How are mammals alike?

heron

Birds

Birds are another group of animals. A heron is a bird. A **bird** has feathers that cover the skin on its body. A bird also has wings. A heron mother lays eggs. Chicks hatch from the eggs.

Make a Model

Use chenille sticks to make a model of a bird or a mammal. Ask a classmate to guess which animal you made. Tell why you made the model as you did.

blue jays

A blue jay is a bird, too. It has feathers and wings that it uses to fly. A blue jay mother lays eggs.

A penguin is also a bird. It has feathers and wings, but it cannot fly. It uses its wings as flippers to swim. A penguin mother lays one egg. The father keeps the egg warm until the new penguin hatches.

Birds are the only animals that have feathers. Birds have wings, and they lay eggs to have young.

penguins

COMPARE AND CONTRAST
How are birds alike?

Mammals and Birds Are Different

This chart lists some details about four animals. Talk about the information it shows.

Mammals and Birds

animal	body covering	how it has its young	what it feeds its young	where it lives
	fur	live	milk from mother's body	land
	feathers	eggs	food that parents find	land
	some hair	live	milk from mother's body	water
	feathers	eggs	food that parents find	land

COMPARE AND CONTRAST

How are mammals and birds different?

What are mammals and birds?

In this lesson, you learned about mammals and birds. You learned how they are alike and how they are different.

1.  **COMPARE AND CONTRAST** Make a chart like this one. Tell how mammals and birds are alike and how they are different.

```
 alike ——— different
```

2. VOCABULARY Use the word **mammal** to tell about this picture.

3. DRAW CONCLUSIONS An animal has fur. What kind of animal is it?

4. SUMMARIZE Use the chart to write a summary of this lesson.

Test Prep

5. You see an animal that flies. It also has feathers. What can you tell about this animal?

    A It is a mammal.

    B It is a bird.

    C It drinks milk.

    D It lives in water.

Make Connections

 Writing

Animal Information

Draw a picture of a mammal or a bird. Write its name, whether it is a mammal or a bird, what its body covering is, and where it lives. Share your work with your classmates.

animal	robin
kind of animal	bird
body covering	feathers
where it lives	park

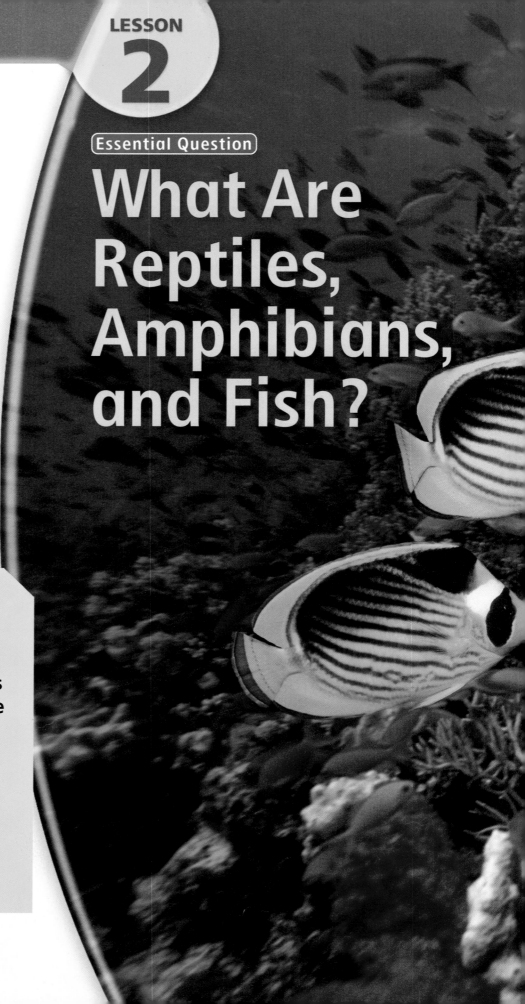

Investigate to find out how to classify animals.

Read and Learn about reptiles, amphibians, and fish.

Essential Question

What Are Reptiles, Amphibians, and Fish?

Fast Fact

Classifying Animals

There are more kinds of fish than there are kinds of mammals, birds, reptiles, and amphibians all put together. You can classify, or sort, animals to better understand all the kinds there are.

fish swimming around a reef

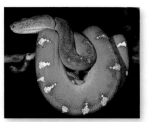

A **reptile** is a member of the group of animals with dry skin that is covered in scales. (p. 94)

An **amphibian** is a member of the group of animals with smooth, wet skin. Young amphibians live in the water, and most adult amphibians live on land. (p. 96)

A **fish** is a member of the group of animals that live in the water and get oxygen through gills. Fish have scales and use fins to swim. (p. 97)

Classify Animals

Guided Inquiry

Ask a Question

Look at the two frogs in this picture. How are they alike? How are they different? Investigate to find out. Then read and learn to find out more.

Get Ready

Inquiry Skill Tip

When you classify animals, it helps you see how they are alike and how they are different.

You need

animal picture sorting cards

index cards

What to Do

Step 1

Observe the animals. How are they alike? How are they different?

Step 2

Classify the animals into groups. The animals in each group should be alike in some way.

Step 3

Write a label for each group. Tell how the animals in the group are alike.

Draw Conclusions

Can you tell how the animals in each group are different?

Independent Inquiry

Classifying animals helps you see how they are alike and how they are different. Classify the animals into five groups.

VOCABULARY
reptile
amphibian
fish

COMPARE AND CONTRAST

Look for ways in which reptiles, amphibians, and fish are alike. Look for ways in which they are different.

Reptiles

A lizard is a reptile. A **reptile** has dry skin covered with scales. Most reptiles walk on four legs. Most reptile mothers lay eggs.

lizard

corn snake

94

A snake is a reptile. Like a lizard, it has dry, scaly skin. Unlike a lizard, a snake has no legs. Most snake mothers lay eggs, but some give birth to live young.

A turtle is a reptile. It has dry, scaly skin. A turtle is the only reptile that has a shell. Some turtles live on land and have legs and feet. Other turtles live in the water. Many water turtles have flippers instead of feet. Turtle mothers lay eggs on land.

turtle

Reptiles are the only animals with dry, scaly skin. What other reptiles can you name?

COMPARE AND CONTRAST

How are reptiles alike?

Snake Skin

Different kinds of snakes have different colors and markings on their skin. Use a hand lens to look at the skin of the snake shown on this page. Draw what you see.

Amphibians

A frog is an amphibian. An **amphibian** has smooth, wet skin. The young hatch from eggs. They live in water. Most adult amphibians live on land.

A salamander is an amphibian. Its skin is smooth and wet. Most salamander mothers lay their eggs in water. Most adult salamanders live on land.

Most amphibians have smooth, wet skin. Young amphibians live in water and take in oxygen through gills. Most adult amphibians live on land and breathe with lungs.

Focus Skill COMPARE AND CONTRAST

How are amphibians alike?

frog

salamander

shark

angelfish

Fish

An angelfish is a fish. A **fish** lives in water and takes in oxygen through gills. It has scales that cover its body. It uses its fins to swim. An angelfish mother lays many eggs.

A shark is a fish. It takes in oxygen through gills and has scales. Its large, strong fins help it swim fast. A shark mother gives birth to live young.

All fish live in water and take in oxygen through gills. Most fish have scales and fins.

COMPARE AND CONTRAST
How are fish alike?

Reptiles, Amphibians, and Fish Are Different

This chart lists some details about four animals. Talk about the information it shows.

Reptiles, Amphibians, and Fish

animal	body covering	how it has its young	where it lives	how it takes in oxygen
	dry, scaly skin	eggs or live	land	lungs
	dry, scaly skin; shell	eggs	land or water	lungs
	smooth, wet skin	eggs	water when young, land as adult	gills when young, lungs as adult
	skin and scales	eggs	water	gills

Focus Skill **COMPARE AND CONTRAST**

How are reptiles, amphibians, and fish different?

Essential Question

What are reptiles, amphibians, and fish?

In this lesson, you learned about reptiles, amphibians, and fish. You learned how they are alike and how they are different.

1. **Focus Skill** **COMPARE AND CONTRAST**
Make a chart like this one. Tell how reptiles, amphibians, and fish are alike and how they are different.

2. **VOCABULARY** Tell about **reptiles**, **amphibians**, and **fish**.

3. **DRAW CONCLUSIONS** Are reptiles more like fish or more like amphibians? Explain your answer.

4. **SUMMARIZE** Use the chart to write two sentences that summarize the lesson.

Test Prep

5. How can you tell whether an animal is a reptile or an amphibian?

Make Connections

 **Math**

Make a Bar Graph

The length of an animal's life is called its life span. The giant tortoise has the longest life span of any animal. The chart shows some animal life spans. Use the data to make a bar graph.

Animal Life Spans

animal	life span
giant tortoise	150 years
alligator	70 years
elephant	70 years
cat	20 years
goldfish	10 years

Investigate to find out how to sequence animals' lives.

Read and Learn about animal life cycles.

What Are Some Animal Life Cycles?

Fast Fact

Animals Change

A newborn bison weighs about as much as a seven-year-old child. Animals grow and change. To see how, you can sequence, or put in order, pictures of their lives.

A **life cycle** is all the stages of the life of a living thing, such as a plant or an animal. (p. 104)

A **tadpole** is a young frog. Tadpoles hatch from eggs and use gills to get oxygen from water. (p. 106)

a newborn bison with an adult bison

101

Sequence Animals' Lives

Guided Inquiry

Ask a Question

This dog has puppies. Are the puppies the same? How will they change as they grow? Investigate to find out. Then read and learn to find out more.

Get Ready

You need

picture sorting cards

What to Do

Step ①

Sort the pictures. Put all the pictures of the same animal in a group.

Step ②

Sequence, or put in order, each group of picture cards. Show how each animal changes as it grows.

Step ③

Tell why you put your cards in the sequence you did.

Draw Conclusions

How would you sequence a person's life?

Independent Inquiry

When you sequence things, you put them in order. Sequence what happens first, next, and last in an animal's life.

VOCABULARY
life cycle
tadpole

 **SEQUENCE**

Look for what happens first, next, then, and last in each animal's life cycle.

The Life Cycle of a Cat

Every animal has a life cycle. A **life cycle** is all the parts of an animal's life. It begins with a new living thing. When the living thing has its own young, a new life cycle begins.

Young mammals start growing inside their mothers' bodies. Kittens grow inside the mother cat. When the kittens are big enough, they are born.

A newborn kitten is helpless. Its mother must care for it. The mother keeps the kitten safe and clean.

2 kitten about 3 weeks old

1 cat and kittens

Like all mammal mothers, the mother cat feeds her kittens with milk from her body. The milk helps the kittens grow.

The kittens get bigger and stronger. As a kitten grows up, it begins to look more like its parents.

After about one year, the cat is fully grown. It can have kittens of its own.

Focus Skill SEQUENCE What happens first, next, then, and last as a cat grows?

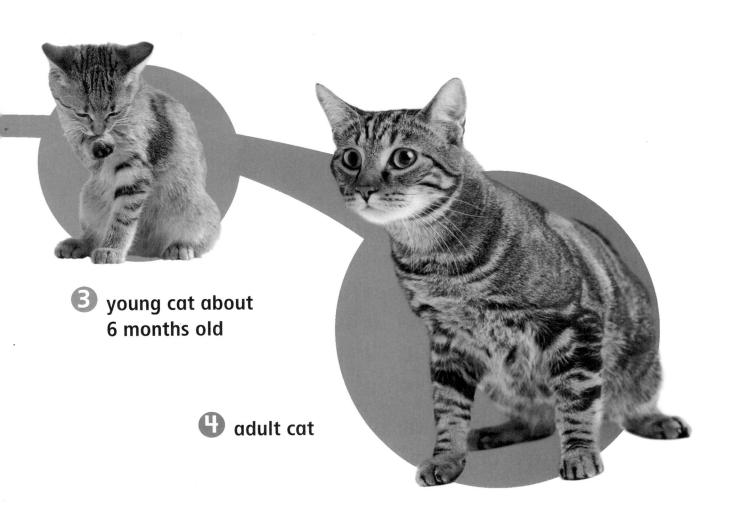

❸ young cat about 6 months old

❹ adult cat

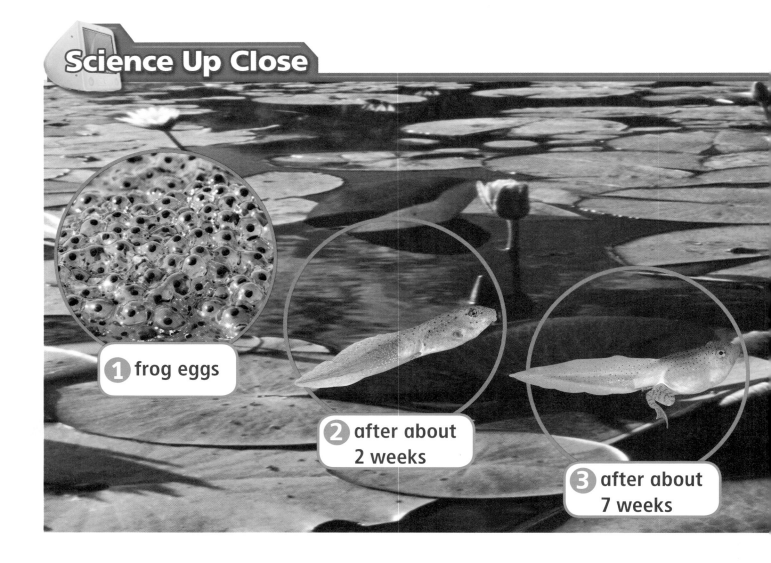

1 frog eggs

2 after about 2 weeks

3 after about 7 weeks

The Life Cycle of a Frog

The life cycle of a frog is different from the life cycles of most other animals. First, a **tadpole**, or young frog, hatches from an egg. A tadpole lives in water. It uses its gills to take in oxygen and its tail to swim. It does not yet look like its parents.

Next, the tadpole eats water plants and insects. It gets bigger and grows two back legs.

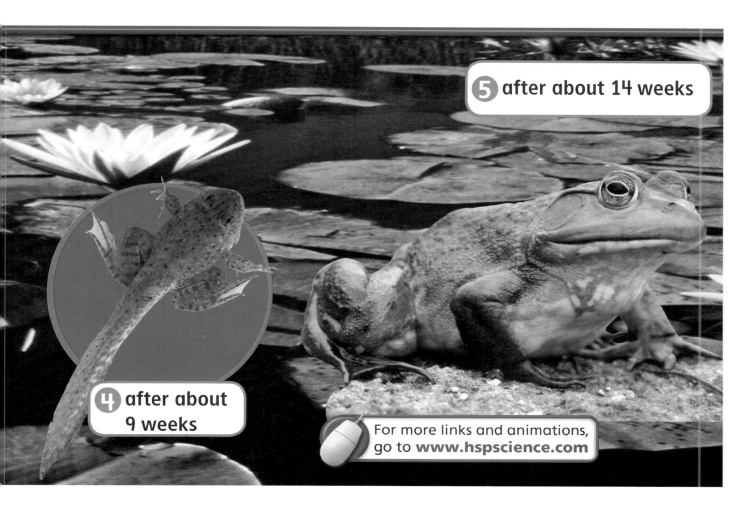

5 after about 14 weeks

4 after about
9 weeks

For more links and animations,
go to **www.hspscience.com**

Then, the tadpole starts
to look more like a frog. It
still has a tail, and now it also
has four legs. It uses lungs to
breathe.

Last, the frog is fully grown
and has no tail. The frog looks
like its parents. It lives on land
most of the time. It can have
its own young.

SEQUENCE What happens first,
next, then, and last as a frog grows?

Insta-Lab

A Dragonfly's Life Cycle

Look at the three
picture cards that show a
dragonfly's life cycle. Put
them in the sequence in
which they happen. Why
did you put the cards in the
order you did?

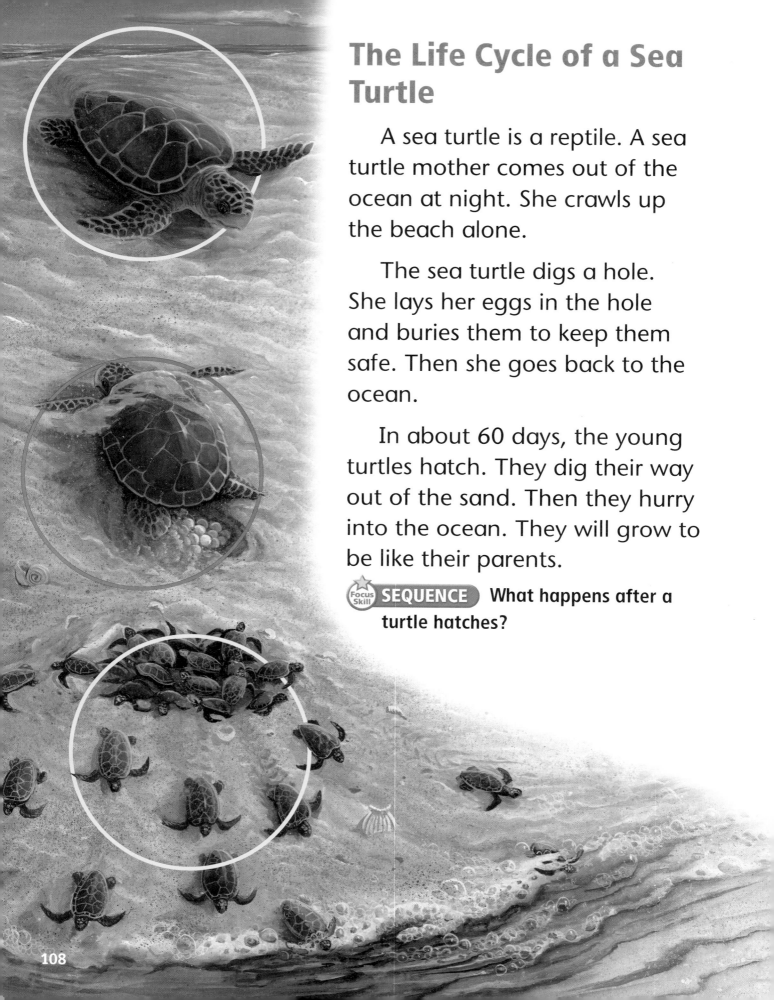

The Life Cycle of a Sea Turtle

A sea turtle is a reptile. A sea turtle mother comes out of the ocean at night. She crawls up the beach alone.

The sea turtle digs a hole. She lays her eggs in the hole and buries them to keep them safe. Then she goes back to the ocean.

In about 60 days, the young turtles hatch. They dig their way out of the sand. Then they hurry into the ocean. They will grow to be like their parents.

Focus Skill **SEQUENCE** **What happens after a turtle hatches?**

Essential Question

What are some animal life cycles?

In this lesson, you learned about the life cycles of some different animals.

1.  **SEQUENCE**
   Make a chart like this one. Tell what happens first, next, then, and last in the life cycle of a frog.

2. **VOCABULARY** Explain the meanings of the terms **life cycle** and **tadpole**.

3. **DRAW CONCLUSIONS** How are the life cycle of a turtle and the life cycle of a frog the same?

4. **SUMMARIZE** Use the chart to write a summary of the lesson.

Test Prep

5. Which is the correct sequence of a life cycle?

   A tadpole, frog, egg

   B one-month-old puppy, newborn puppy, dog

   C egg, young sea turtle, adult sea turtle

   D egg, frog, tadpole

Make Connections

 Art

Model an Animal's Life Cycle

Choose an animal. Use clay to model the stages of that animal's life cycle.

JoAnne Simerson

To some people, JoAnne Simerson has the greatest job in the world. Simerson works in a zoo. She is an expert on animal behavior.

Simerson works with many kinds of animals. Her favorites are big mammals like polar bears. In the wild, polar bears play games with one another. In the zoo, Simerson encourages the bears to do the same thing. She gives the bears different toys. The bears need to play so they stay active and learn new things.

► **JOANNE SIMERSON**
► Works with animals

 Think and Write

Why is learning about animal behavior important?

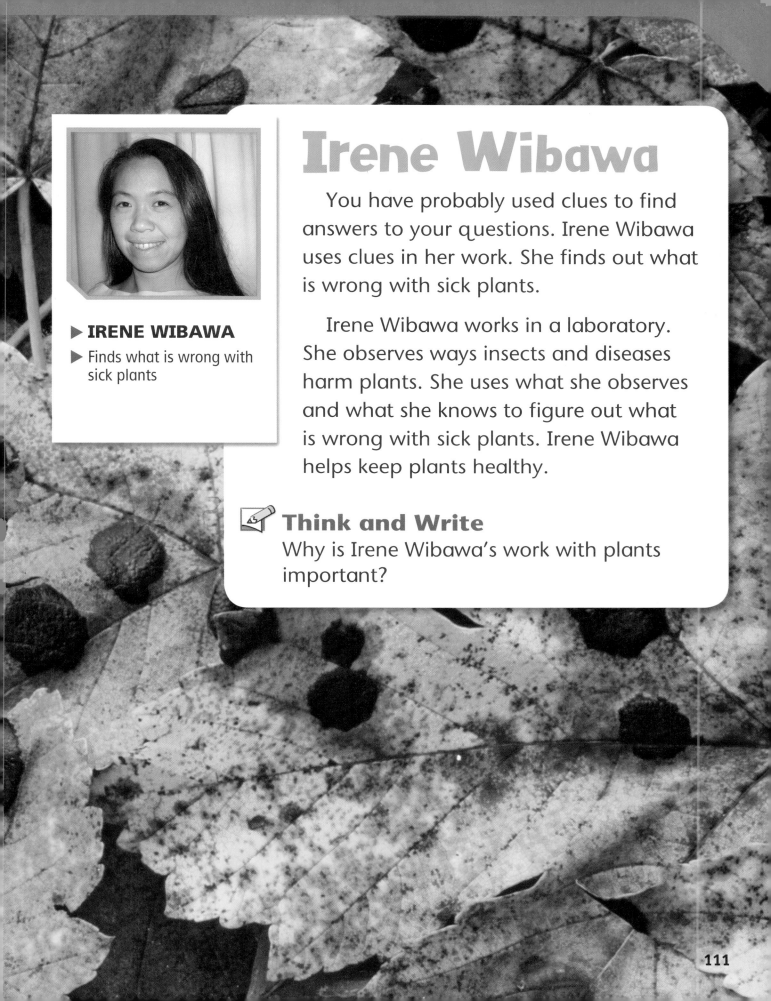

Irene Wibawa

You have probably used clues to find answers to your questions. Irene Wibawa uses clues in her work. She finds out what is wrong with sick plants.

Irene Wibawa works in a laboratory. She observes ways insects and diseases harm plants. She uses what she observes and what she knows to figure out what is wrong with sick plants. Irene Wibawa helps keep plants healthy.

▶ **IRENE WIBAWA**
▶ Finds what is wrong with sick plants

Think and Write

Why is Irene Wibawa's work with plants important?

Vocabulary Review

Use the terms to complete the sentences. The page numbers tell you where to look if you need help.

mammal p. 84   **amphibian** p. 96

bird p. 86   **life cycle** p. 104

reptile p. 94   **tadpole** p. 106

1. An animal with fur or hair is a _____.

2. A young frog is a _____.

3. An animal with dry, scaly skin is a _____.

4. An animal with smooth, wet skin is an _____.

5. All the stages of an animal's life are its _____.

6. An animal that has feathers and lays eggs is a _____.

Check Understanding

7. Write **first**, **next**, **then**, and **last** to show the sequence.

8. How are these animals alike?

    A Both lay eggs.

    B Both have shells.

    C Both are reptiles.

    D They are both nonliving things.

Critical Thinking

Adam observes some birds in a tree.

9. What is happening in each picture?

The **Big Idea**

10. Write about and draw another animal's life cycle.

Plants have parts that help them live and grow.

GO online → Student eBook
www.hspscience.com

What will happen to these dandelion seeds after they reach the ground? How does this connect to the **Big Idea?**

Investigate to find out about parts of a plant.

Read and Learn about what the parts of a plant are.

Essential Question

What Are the Parts of a Plant?

Fast Fact

Vines

Grapes grow on weak stems called vines. Vines can not hold up their leaves and flowers, as most stems do. Many vines have parts that help them hold onto something for support. You can learn about plants by observing them.

Roots are the parts of a plant that take in water and nutrients. Most roots grow underground and help hold the plant in place. (p. 120)

Stems are the parts of a plant that carry water and nutrients from the roots to the leaves. (p. 120)

Leaves are the parts of a plant that make food for the plant. Leaves use light, a gas in air, and water to make food. (p. 121)

Flowers are the parts of some plants that help them make new plants. Part of the flower makes seeds that grow into new plants. (p. 121)

117

Parts of a Plant

Ask a Question

An oak tree is starting to grow. What can you observe? Can you name the plant parts you see? Investigate to find out. Then read and learn to find out more.

Get Ready

Inquiry Skill Tip
You can use your senses of sight, smell, and touch to observe plants.

You need

2 carnations

2 clear cups of colored water

What to Do

Step ① —

Bend the stem of one carnation.

Step ② —

Put each carnation in a cup of colored water.

Step ③

Observe the carnations for two days.

Draw Conclusions

What changes do you see?

Independent Inquiry

When you **observe**, you can use your senses of sight and smell. Observe what happens to a flower when the stem is cut and put into different colors of water.

119

Parts of a Plant

Plants need sunlight, air, water, and nutrients from the soil to grow. Each part of a plant helps the plant get the things it needs.

Roots take in water and nutrients from the soil. Some roots also store food for plants. Most plants, such as this rose plant, have roots that grow underground. They help hold the plant in the ground.

Stems carry water and nutrients from the roots to the leaves. Most stems also help hold up the plant so it can get light.

rose plant

stem

roots

flower

leaf

Leaves make food for the plant. They use light, a gas in air, and water to make the food.

Flowers help plants make new plants. Part of the flower makes seeds that grow into new plants.

Focus Skill MAIN IDEA AND DETAILS

What parts of a plant help it grow?

Insta-Lab

Make a Model

Show how a stem holds up the flower and the leaves of a plant. Use chenille sticks, colored paper, and tape to make a model. Tell why a stem is important.

Parts of a Flower

petals with pollen

fruit with seeds

Flowers are made up of many parts. The petals are usually the colorful parts. The pollen is like a powder. Pollen helps the plant make seeds. A fruit grows around the seeds to hold and protect them.

 MAIN IDEA AND DETAILS What are some parts of a flower?

 For more links and animations, go to **www.hspscience.com**

Essential Question

What are the parts of a plant?

In this lesson, you learned about different parts of a plant and how those parts help the plant live and grow.

1. Focus Skill **MAIN IDEA AND DETAILS**
Make a chart like this one. Fill in details about this main idea. **Each part of a plant helps the plant get the things it needs to live.**

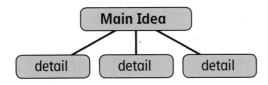

2. VOCABULARY Use the terms **roots**, **stems**, and **leaves** to tell how this plant gets water and how it uses water.

3. DRAW CONCLUSIONS What would happen to a plant if an animal ate all its leaves?

4. SUMMARIZE Write three sentences that tell about the plant parts you learned about in this lesson.

Test Prep

5. How do flowers help make new plants?

Make Connections

 Writing

Plant Riddles
Use four index cards. On each card, write a riddle about a plant part. Write the answer on the back. Trade cards with a partner. Read each riddle, and name the plant part.

I carry water to the leaves. What am I?

I help hold the plant in the ground. What am I?

I help make new plants. What am I?

I make food for the plant. What am I?

Essential Question

How Do Plants Differ?

Investigate to find out how to classify leaves.

Read and Learn about ways plants are different.

Fast Fact

Plant Parts

Some plants have stems that grow partly underground. You can classify plants by looking at their parts.

Vocabulary Preview

A **trunk** is the main stem of a tree. (p. 129)

A **shrub** is a bush. Shrubs have woody stems. (p. 129)

125

Classify Leaves

Guided Inquiry

Ask a Question

These flowers are very colorful. What colors do you see? What are some ways in which the flowers are alike and different? Investigate to find out. Then read and learn to find out more.

Get Ready

Inquiry Skill Tip

When you classify, you sort things by how they are alike.

You need

leaves

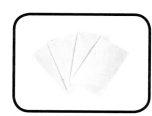

index cards

What to Do

Step ①

Observe the leaves. How are they alike? How are they different?

Step ②

Classify the leaves by grouping leaves that are alike.

Step ③

Write a label for each group of leaves. Tell how the leaves are alike. Tell about leaves you see where you live.

Draw Conclusions

Observe the leaves again. Can you think of another way to sort them?

Independent Inquiry

When you **classify** things, you sort them by how they are alike and how they are different. Classify leaves by looking at their veins.

VOCABULARY
trunk
shrub

 COMPARE AND CONTRAST
Look for ways plants are alike and ways they are different.

Kinds of Leaves

Plants have leaves that are different shapes and sizes. Leaves can be long, short, wide, or narrow. They can be shaped like needles. Some leaves have smooth edges. Others have wavy or pointed edges. Some are divided into parts.

plant

 COMPARE AND CONTRAST How are the fern, spruce, and maple leaves different?

Fern   Spruce   Maple

| Tulip | Cactus | Tree | Bush |

Kinds of Stems

Plants have different kinds of stems. A tree has one main stem called a **trunk**. It is hard and woody. A **shrub**, or bush, is a plant with many woody stems. Other plants, such as tulips, have soft stems. A cactus has a thick stem that stores water.

 **COMPARE AND CONTRAST**
How are stems different?

What Kind of Stem?
Look outside and choose a plant. Does it have a woody stem or a soft stem? Does it have one stem or many stems? Draw a picture of the stem or stems. Describe the plant to a classmate.

Kinds of Roots

Most plants have either one thick main root or many thin roots. The thin roots are usually about the same size.

Carrot plants have one thick root. Tiny, thin roots grow out from it. Corn plants have many thin roots. Smaller roots grow out from them.

Focus Skill **COMPARE AND CONTRAST** How are the roots of carrot plants different from the roots of corn plants?

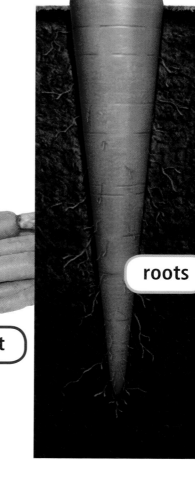

roots

carrot plant

corn plant

roots

How do plants differ?

In this lesson, you learned that different kinds of plants have different leaves, stems, and roots.

1. **Focus Skill** **COMPARE AND CONTRAST** Make a chart like this one. Tell how plants are alike and how they are different.

| alike | — | different |

2. VOCABULARY Use the term **trunk** to tell about a tree.

3. DRAW CONCLUSIONS What would happen to a plant if its roots were damaged?

4. SUMMARIZE Write a sentence that tells the most important idea of this lesson.

Test Prep

5. Which kind of plant has many woody stems?

A flower

B shrub

C tree

D tulip

Make Connections

 **Math**

Measure Lengths of Leaves
Leaves from different kinds of plants are different lengths. Gather leaves from five kinds of plants. Use a ruler to measure the length of each one. Record the information in a chart.

Lengths of Leaves

plant	leaf length
ivy vine	2 inches
maple tree	
pine tree	
lilac bush	

Essential Question

What Are Some Plant Life Cycles?

Investigate to find out about the life cycle of a bean plant.

Read and Learn about plant life cycles.

Fast Fact

Observing Pinecones

When pinecones first grow on a tree, they are soft and green. As pinecones grow they become hard and brown. You can communicate what you observe about how plants change.

A **life cycle** is all the stages of the life of a living thing, such as a plant or an animal. (p. 136)

To **germinate** is to start to grow. A seed may germinate when it gets water, warmth, and oxygen. (p. 136)

watering a pine tree

133

Life Cycle of a Bean Plant

Guided Inquiry

Ask a Question

These beans don't just look good. They taste good, too! Where do the beans people eat come from? Are all beans brown?

Investigate to find out. Then read and learn to find out more.

Get Ready

Inquiry Skill Tip

You can use pictures to help you communicate about things you observe.

You need

cup filled with soil

pencil

beans

water

What to Do

Step ①

Use the pencil to make holes in the soil. Put a bean in each hole. Cover the beans with soil.

Step ②

Water the soil. Put the cup in a warm, sunny place.

Step ③

Observe the cup each day for two weeks. Water the soil when it is dry. Draw what you observe. **Communicate** what is happening.

Draw Conclusions

When the bean plant was growing what changes did you observe?

Independent Inquiry

You can use pictures and words to help you **communicate**. Communicate how much a bean plant grows.

VOCABULARY
life cycle
germinate

 SEQUENCE
Look for the order of the stages of a plant's life cycle.

Life Cycle of a Bean Plant

All the stages of a plant's life make up its **life cycle**. A plant's life cycle begins with a seed. First, the seed germinates, or begins to grow. Next, the seed grows into a mature, or adult, plant. Then, the plant makes seeds that may grow into new plants.

Inside each bean seed is a tiny plant and some stored food. The plant uses the food when it begins to grow.

When a seed gets water, warmth, and oxygen from the air, it may germinate, or start to grow. The root grows down.

Last, a new life cycle begins. Different kinds of plants have different life cycles.

Focus Skill **SEQUENCE** What happens after a bean seed germinates?

The stem of the tiny plant breaks through the ground. It grows up toward the light. It starts making food that the plant uses to keep growing.

More leaves and stems grow. Flowers will grow on the bean plant and make seeds.

Life Cycle of a Pine Tree

A pine tree's life cycle begins with a seed. But pine trees do not have flowers and fruits that hold seeds. Instead, they make seeds in cones.

Focus Skill **SEQUENCE** What happens after a pinecone makes seeds?

Next, the seeds germinate. After the new plants grow a little, they look like small pine trees.

Pinecones hold and protect the pine seeds until they are ready to grow. Then the pinecones open up. The wind blows the seeds, and they fall to the ground.

Over time, the pine tree gets taller. More branches and needles grow. The trunk gets thicker. Pinecones grow on the tree. Last, the pinecones make seeds. A new life cycle begins.

Insta-Lab

Observe a Pinecone

Use a hand lens to look at a pinecone or a picture of one. Observe the scales that make up a pinecone. Describe a pinecone to a classmate. Tell why you think the pinecone has scales.

Plants Look Like Their Parents

Plants make new plants that look very much like them. At first, the new plant may look different. Later, it grows the same kind of leaves, stems, and flowers or cones as the plant it came from.

An oak tree grows from a seed inside an acorn. The seed grows into a small plant. The plant grows and changes until it looks like an oak tree.

Even though the new tree is like its parent, the new tree can look a little different. When the new tree is grown, it may be taller or shorter than the parent tree. The new tree may have more or fewer branches and smaller or larger leaves.

Focus Skill SEQUENCE What happens as young plants grow and change?

palm tree and coconut

oak tree

acorn

140

What are some plant life cycles?

In this lesson, you learned about the life cycles of different plants.

1.  **SEQUENCE**
Make a chart like this one. Show the life cycle of a bean plant.

☐ → ☐ → ☐

2. VOCABULARY
Explain the meanings of the terms **life cycle** and **germinate**.

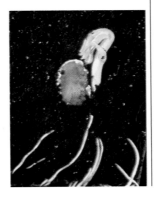

3. DRAW CONCLUSIONS How are flowers and pinecones alike?

4. SUMMARIZE Use the chart to write sentences that tell what this lesson is mostly about. Use the words **first**, **next**, **then**, and **last**.

Test Prep

5. What will a seed grow into? How do you know?

Make Connections

 Physical Education

A Germinating Seed
Pretend you are the tiny plant inside a seed. Use your body to show how the seed opens and the tiny plant begins to grow.

Making a Difference

Children in Clarksville, Tennessee, have green thumbs. But they did not paint their thumbs green. We say they have green thumbs because they planted more than 100 trees.

The kids planted the trees as part of Make a Difference Day. The newspaper *USA Today* started Make a Difference Day more than 14 years ago.

On Make a Difference Day, millions of people do something nice for their communities. Three million people took part in a recent Make a Difference Day.

Idea Generator

Planting Trees

The children in Clarksville had to work hard to plant 125 trees. The trees were about 10 to 12 inches tall when they were planted.

The trees will be good for the community. They will give lots of shade to block the sun. People will enjoy the shade in the summer because it can get very hot in Tennessee.

The trees will also become homes for birds and help keep the air clean.

If kids and their families want to help but do not know what to do, they can turn to the Idea Generator. This is a website run by *USA Today*. After a person answers three questions, the Idea Generator comes up with ideas for Make a Difference projects.

Think and Write
Can you think of other ways that trees help a community?

Find out more. Log on to
www.hspscience.com

Vocabulary Review

Match each term with the picture that shows its meaning. The page numbers tell where to look if you need help.

roots p. 120   **leaves** p. 121

stems p. 120   **flowers** p. 121

1. _____

2. _____

3. _____

4. _____

Check Understanding

5. Write **first**, **next**, **then**, and **last** to show the sequence.

_____ _____ _____ _____

6. Which sentence gives a correct detail about plants?

    A Flowers make seeds.

    B Stems make pollen.

    C Roots make food for the plant.

    D Leaves grow underground.

Critical Thinking

7. Why is the root the first part of a plant to grow?

The Big Idea

8. Jeanie has a plant that does not look healthy. The soil around the plant looks very dry. What should Jeanie do? Why?

Tell how each picture shows the **Big Idea** for its chapter.

CHAPTER 1

Big Idea
Living things have needs and change as they grow.

Big Idea
There are many kinds of animals. Animals can be grouped by their traits.

Big Idea
Plants have parts that help them live and grow.

Homes for Living Things

UNIT
B
LIFE SCIENCE

Unit Inquiry

Water Pollution

As you do this unit, you will learn about homes that are safe for living things. Plan and do a test. See what happens when you pollute the water needed by a plant.

4 Living Things in Their Environments

Different areas have places where plants and animals find the things they need, such as food, water, and shelter.

Go online
Student eBook
www.hspscience.com

What do yOU wonder?

Why might these elephants have gone to this area to live in? Think about the **Big Idea** to help you answer.

elephants at a watering hole

LESSON

1

Essential Question

What Is An Environment?

Investigate to find out about how energy flows.

Read and Learn about environments.

Fast Fact

Animal homes
Alligators live in lakes, ponds, and rivers. They can hide in the water while they hunt for food. You can draw conclusions to figure out why animals live in certain places.

An **environment** is a place and all the living and nonliving things in it. (p. 154)

A **habitat** is a place where a living thing can get the food, water, and shelter it needs to live. (p. 155)

To **adapt** is to change. Kinds of animals and plants adapt over time to live in their environments. (p. 157)

Energy Flow

Guided Inquiry

Ask a Question

Energy helps this plant grow. Where is the energy coming from? Investigate to find out. Then read and learn to find out more.

Get Ready

You need

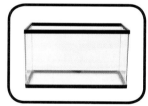

glass tank with pebbles and soil

water

small plants and worms

What to Do

Step ①

Make a model to show how living things get energy. Put pebbles in the bottom of a glass tank. Put soil on top of the pebbles.

Step ②

Add plants. Water the soil. Place worms in the tank.

Step ③

Observe the tank each day. What changes do you see?

Draw Conclusions

How do the living things get energy?

Independent Inquiry

When you **make a model**, you can show how plants and animals get energy. Observe your model. Draw the changes you see.

MAIN IDEA AND DETAILS

Look for details about where animals and plants live.

Environments and Habitats

An **environment** is made up of all the living and nonliving things in a place. Animals and plants are the living things. Water, weather, and rocks are some of the nonliving things. Environments can be hot or cold. They can be wet or dry. Animals and plants from one environment often can not live in another one.

An environment is made up of different habitats. A **habitat** is a place where living things have food and water and the kind of shelter they need. In a forest environment, a pond is a habitat for fish. Part of the forest may be a habitat for birds. What habitats do you see in this picture?

MAIN IDEA AND DETAILS

What do animals and plants need in a habitat?

People and Environments

People can change environments. They may cut down trees and clear away other plants to build houses. When they do this, animals can lose their habitats.

Environments also change when people bring in new plants or animals. People brought water hyacinths to Florida.

The water hyacinths grew quickly and covered the water. They shut out air and light. The other plants began to die. The hyacinths used all the oxygen in the water. Then the fish died.

Focus Skill) MAIN IDEA AND DETAILS What can happen when people change environments?

water hyacinths

sea otters

red pigfish

How Animals and Plants Adapt

Over time, animals and plants **adapt**, or change, to be able to live in their environment. They adapt in different ways to meet their needs. A fish has gills to take in oxygen from water. An otter has fur to keep it warm.

Focus Skill MAIN IDEA AND DETAILS

Why do plants and animals adapt?

Insta-Lab

How Feathers Help Ducks

Cut out two paper feathers. Cover both sides of one feather with margarine. Dip both feathers into a bowl of water. Which one does not soak up water? Why do you think ducks have an oily coating on their feathers?

Beaks and Teeth

Animals' beaks and teeth are adapted to help them get food.

You can tell what kind of food a bird eats by looking at the shape of its beak.

eats insects

eats small seeds

eats big seeds

You can tell what kind of food a mammal eats by looking at its teeth.

horse— eats plants

tiger— eats meat

bear—eats plants and meat

For more links and animations, go to **www.hspscience.com**

What is an environment?

In this lesson, you learned about environments and habitats.

1. 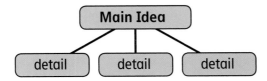 **MAIN IDEA AND DETAILS**
Make a chart like this one. Fill in details about this main idea. **An environment is made up of living and nonliving things.**

```
        ┌──────────────┐
        │  Main Idea   │
        └──────────────┘
       ╱       │       ╲
┌────────┐ ┌────────┐ ┌────────┐
│ detail │ │ detail │ │ detail │
└────────┘ └────────┘ └────────┘
```

2. VOCABULARY Use the term **adapt** to tell about this picture.

3. DRAW CONCLUSIONS What might an animal do if it could not find water in its habitat?

4. SUMMARIZE Use the chart to write a summary of the lesson.

Test Prep

5. Which are nonliving things in an environment?

A air and plants
B animals and air
C plants and water
D water and rocks

Make Connections

 Writing

Description of an Environment
Choose an animal. Describe its environment. Then draw a picture of the animal in its environment. Share your work with a classmate.

Investigate to find out how color helps a butterfly.

Read and Learn about how living things survive in different places.

How Do Living Things Survive in Different Places?

Fast Fact

Animal Hiding
Some animals stay safe by blending in with their environment. Making inferences will help you figure out how animals stay safe.

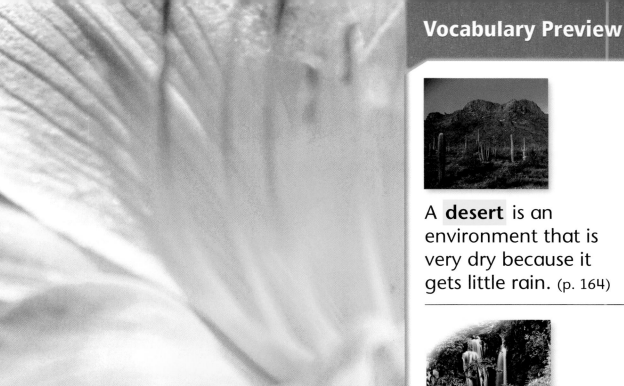

A **desert** is an environment that is very dry because it gets little rain. (p. 164)

A **rain forest** is an environment with many tall trees that gets rain almost every day. (p. 165)

A **grassland** is an open environment covered with grass. (p. 166)

A **tundra** is an environment that is cold and snowy. (p. 167)

An **ocean** is a large body of salt water. (p. 168)

A **pond** is a small freshwater environment. (p. 170)

How Color Helps a Butterfly

Guided Inquiry

Ask a Question

Color helps this butterfly hide. What might some other animals need in order to hide? Investigate to find out. Then read and learn to find out more.

Get Ready

Inquiry Skill Tip
When you infer, you use what you see to figure out why something happened.

You need

paper squares

orange paper

clock

What to Do

Step ① ────────────

Scatter equal numbers of purple, orange, and yellow squares on the sheet of paper.

Step ② ────────────

Count the purple squares for five seconds. Record the number. Repeat for the orange and yellow squares.

Step ③

Which color squares were hardest to count?

Draw Conclusions

What can you **infer** about how color helps a butterfly?

Independent Inquiry

When you **infer**, you think about what you saw and figure out why it happened. Infer what kinds of environments could help keep different animals safe.

VOCABULARY

desert   tundra
rain forest   ocean
grassland   pond

⭐ **MAIN IDEA AND DETAILS**

Look for details that tell ways animals and plants have adapted to their environments.

Desert

Animals and plants have adapted to the environments they live in.

A **desert** is a dry environment that gets little rain. Few kinds of plants and animals are adapted to living there. A cactus stores water that it can use later. Lizards hide under rocks during the day, when it is hot. They come out to find food at night, when it is cool.

⭐ **MAIN IDEA AND DETAILS** How have plants and animals adapted to living in deserts?

The veiled chameleon eats fruits, flowers, and leaves to get water.

The sharp needles on a saguaro cactus keep away animals that want to eat it.

Rain Forest

A **rain forest** is a wet environment that gets rain almost every day. Many rain forests are also hot all year. They have many tall trees that block the sunlight. Some plants grow high on the trees to reach the light.

Some monkeys live high in the trees, too. They can hold onto branches with their tails. This lets them grab food with their hands. Bats hunt at night, when they can catch flying insects and other small animals.

The green tree frog has sticky feet that help it climb.

 **MAIN IDEA AND DETAILS**

How have plants and animals adapted to living in rain forests?

Cheetahs are the fastest animals on land. The color of gazelles helps them hide from cheetahs. The cheetahs can not easily see the gazelles in the grass.

Grassland

A **grassland** is an open environment that is covered with grass. Few trees grow there, so it is hard for large animals to hide. Elephants and other animals travel in groups of their own kind to stay safe. Some animals are able to run fast. This helps them stay safe.

Focus Skill MAIN IDEA AND DETAILS

How have animals adapted to living in the grassland?

Keeping Warm

Does fat keep animals warm? Place shortening in a plastic bag. Put another plastic bag over each hand. Then put one hand in the bag with the shortening and the other hand in an empty bag. Put both hands in a bowl of cold water. Which hand stays warm longer?

Tundra

A **tundra** is a cold, snowy environment. Plants do not grow very tall, and they grow close together. This helps protect them from the very cold temperatures. Many tundra animals have thick fur to keep them warm. Some animals have fur that changes with the seasons. In spring, new brown fur grows in to help them hide in summer. In fall, white fur grows in to help them hide in winter.

Polar bears stay warm because of their fat and their thick fur.

Focus Skill **MAIN IDEA AND DETAILS**

How have plants and animals adapted to living in the tundra?

Caribou travel from place to place to find the plants they eat.

Ocean

An **ocean** is a large body of salt water. Most ocean plants and animals live in the top layer of the ocean. There, the plants can get the sunlight they need, and the animals can find food.

Ocean animals stay safe in many ways. Some fish change colors to help them hide. Others swim fast or hide in small cracks.

A jellyfish stings other animals that come too close to it.

Focus Skill MAIN IDEA AND DETAILS

How do ocean animals stay safe?

Fish have scales to protect their bodies.

A shark's sharp teeth help it catch food. Its scales and body shape help it swim quickly.

An octopus uses its eight long arms to catch food.

Pond

A **pond** is a small freshwater environment. Water lilies may grow on the surface of a pond. There, they can get the sunlight they need. Many animals, such as beavers, live in ponds. Beavers have webbed feet to help them swim. They use their sharp teeth to cut down trees to build their homes.

Focus Skill MAIN IDEA AND DETAILS

How have plants and animals adapted to living in ponds?

Water striders can walk on the surface of the pond without sinking.

water lilies

Essential Question

How do living things survive in different places?

In this lesson, you learned about different places in which plants and animals live and about how they survive there.

1. **MAIN IDEA AND DETAILS**
Make a chart like this one.
Fill in details about this main
idea. **Plants and animals
have adapted to living
in many environments**.

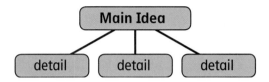

2. **VOCABULARY** Use the terms
desert and **tundra** to tell
about environments.

3. **DRAW CONCLUSIONS** Why
would it be hard for a
rainforest animal to live in a
grassland environment?

4. **SUMMARIZE** Write two
sentences to tell what you
learned in this lesson.

Test Prep

5. What kind of environment
does an animal with webbed
feet probably live in?

  A cold

  B dry

  C warm

  D wet

Make Connections

Math

Solve a Problem
Use this chart to find out how much
more rain falls in a rain forest than
in a desert. How could you solve
the problem without measuring the
difference? Write a math sentence
that shows how.

Average Rainfall in One Month	
desert	2 cm
rain forest	20 cm

Investigate to find out what animals eat.

Read and Learn about food chains and food webs.

Essential Question

What Are Food Chains and Food Webs?

Fast Fact

Animal Food
This great blue heron eats fish. You can communicate what you learn about what animals eat.

A **food chain** is a diagram that shows the order in which living things eat one another. (p. 176)

A **food web** is a diagram that shows how food chains are connected. (p. 178)

173

What Animals Eat

Ask a Question

Animals need food to survive. What is this squirrel eating? Investigate to find out. Then read and learn to find out more.

Get Ready

Inquiry Skill Tip

When you communicate your ideas, you tell what you know.

You need

animal picture sorting cards

books about animals

markers

What to Do

Step ①

Choose a picture of an animal. Find out what that animal eats.

Step ②

Draw and label a picture of the food.

Step ③

Use your pictures and cards to **communicate** your ideas.

Draw Conclusions

What would happen to an animal if it did not have food to eat?

SEQUENCE
Look for the order in which animals eat other living things.

Food Chains

Living things need one another to survive. A **food chain** shows the order in which animals eat plants and other animals.

Food chains start with sunlight and plants. In this food chain, first, the grass uses sunlight to make its food. Second, a grasshopper eats the grass. Third, a frog eats the grasshopper. Fourth, a snake eats the frog. Last, a hawk eats the snake.

SEQUENCE What happens after a grasshopper eats grass?

Food Chain Mix-Up

On three index cards, draw a plant and two animals that all belong in the same food chain. Mix up the cards, and ask a partner to put them in the right order. Have your partner explain how the food chain works.

Food Webs

Most animals eat more than one kind of food. So an animal may be part of more than one food chain. Connected food chains are called a **food web**. Look at this food web. Use the arrows to find out the foods each animal eats.

Focus Skill **SEQUENCE** What happens after the frog eats the grasshopper?

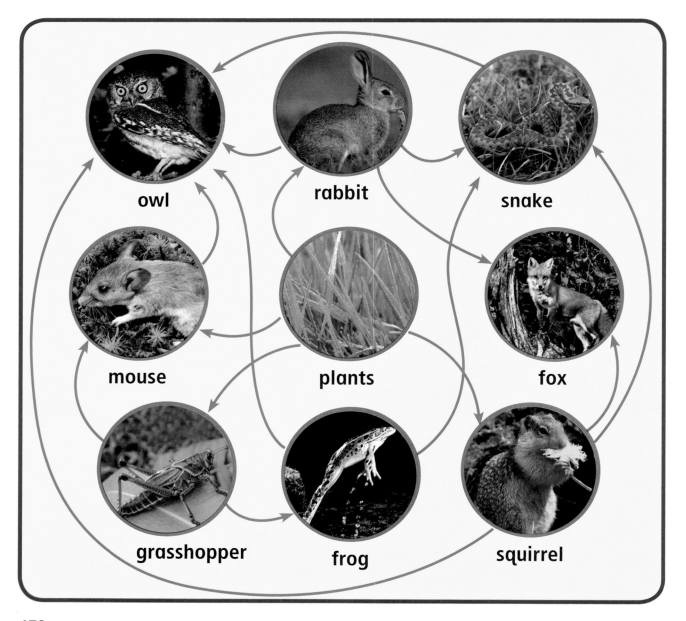

owl

rabbit

snake

mouse

plants

fox

grasshopper

frog

squirrel

Essential Question

What are food chains and food webs?

In this lesson, you learned about food chains and food webs.

1. **SEQUENCE**
Make a chart like this one.
Show a food chain.

2. **VOCABULARY** Explain the difference between a **food chain** and a **food web**.

3. **DRAW CONCLUSIONS** What would happen if one part of a food web were missing?

4. **SUMMARIZE** Write two sentences that tell what this lesson is about.

Test Prep

5. Which is a food chain?

   A plant, fox, mouse

   B seeds, squirrel, fox

   C snake, seeds, frog

   D grasshopper, frog, plant

Make Connections

 Art

Food Web Mobile

On index cards, draw and label plants and animals that make up a food web. Punch a hole in the top, the bottom, and both sides of each card. Connect the cards with yarn to show how the food web works. Then hang the cards from a hanger.

Helping HAWAI'I'S Reefs

In Hawai`i, coral reefs surround the islands. The reefs have been damaged by people and ships.

But there is help for the reefs. The United States government has passed laws to help protect the reefs around Hawai`i.

What Are Coral Reefs?

A coral reef is made up of the skeletons of tiny sea animals. A reef is often found in warm, shallow waters. More than half the United States' coral reefs are located in the waters around Hawai`i.

Coral reefs provide homes for other sea animals. Reefs also protect coastlines from dangerous waves. When waves pass over reefs, they slow down and get smaller.

How Are Reefs Formed?

A coral reef is built by tiny sea creatures called coral polyps. When coral polyps die, their hard outer skeletons stay and other polyps grow on top of the skeletons. After a long time, the coral skeletons build up, forming a reef.

A reef can also be formed by people. For example, people have made several reefs by sinking ships or even subway cars. These reefs then provide shelter for fish and a place for underwater plants to grow.

✎ Think and Write

How do coral reefs help fish to survive?

coral

Vocabulary Review

Match each term with the picture that shows its meaning. The page numbers tell you where to look if you need help.

desert p. 164   **tundra** p. 167

rain forest p. 165   **ocean** p. 168

grassland p. 166   **pond** p. 170

1. _____

2. _____

3. _____

4. _____

5. _____

6. _____

Check Understanding

7. What is always at the beginning of a food chain?

A fish

B sunlight and plants

C owls

D trees and birds

8. In which kind of environment do caribou and polar bears live?

F cold

G dry

H hot

J wet

Critical Thinking

9. These pictures show what an arctic fox looks like in winter and in summer.

Tell how the fox has adapted to living in its environment.

10. What might happen to a food web if a new kind of animal came to live in an environment?

The **Big Idea**

Visual Summary

Tell how each picture shows the **Big Idea** for the chapter.

Big Idea

Different areas have places where plants and animals find the things they need such as food, water, and shelter.

EARTH SCIENCE

PENNSYLVANIA

Pittsburgh

Carnegie Museum of Natural History

fossils at the museum

The world was very different long ago. Places that are dry now were once wet. Places that were low are now high. Things that lived once are gone forever. One way to find out more about these times is by looking at fossils. At this museum, you can see many fossils. There is much more to see, too!

The Many Parts of the Museum

This museum is a great place to find out about the natural world. You can see rocks and gems from Pennsylvania and from around the world. You can look at plants that grow in Pennsylvania. You can see animals from all over the world, too. You can find out more about Earth.

The PaleoLab

People work on fossils at the lab. They clean fossils, fit pieces of fossils together, and date fossils. Then they put the fossils out for people to see.

The lab workers help visitors learn about the past. They can find out what lived long ago and how the world was different. They can learn how life has changed on Earth.

Think And Write

1. **Scientific Thinking** How can fossils tell us more about the world long ago?

2. **Scientific Thinking** What tools might the workers in the PaleoLab use?

Planetarium
at the
Reading Public Museum

If you want to know more about the stars, this is the place for you. You can learn about the stars and find out what else is out in space. You can find where Earth is in our solar system.

What's in a Planetarium?

In the planetarium, you can sit back and see on the ceiling a show about space. You might take a trip around the stars or visit the planets. You can find out where the planets and the sun are located. As you watch, you can hear a voice telling you what you are seeing.

A Trip to Space

As you travel, the show tells about the search for water in space. Without water, there would be no life on Earth. In this show, you can find out how scientists look for water on other planets.

Earth from space

Think And Write

1. **Scientific Thinking** What are some questions you have about space that the planetarium might answer?

2. **Scientific Thinking** How does a planetarium show where Earth is in space?

Farmington

FALLINGWATER

Fallingwater is one of the best-known houses in the world. It is in the western part of Pennsylvania. The house was built in the 1930s. Frank Lloyd Wright designed it. It juts out over a stream. It looks a little like water falling. Wright knew that the family building the house loved the stream. That is why he designed their house this way. Today, people travel from many states and countries to see this house.

working on Fallingwater

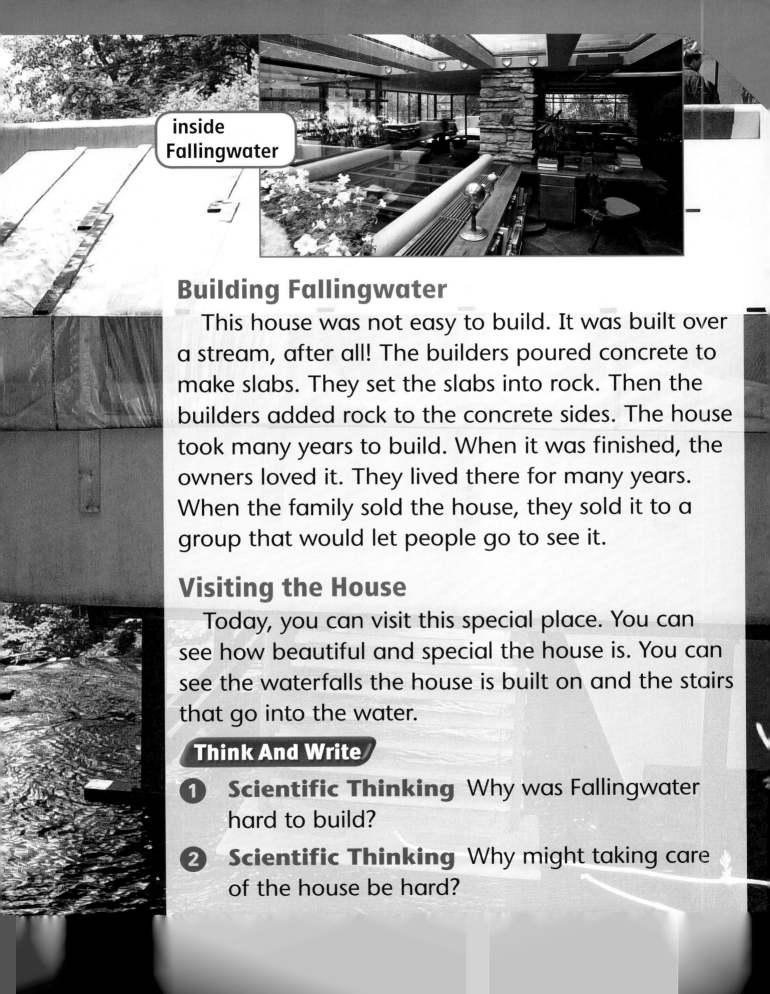

inside
Fallingwater

Building Fallingwater

This house was not easy to build. It was built over a stream, after all! The builders poured concrete to make slabs. They set the slabs into rock. Then the builders added rock to the concrete sides. The house took many years to build. When it was finished, the owners loved it. They lived there for many years. When the family sold the house, they sold it to a group that would let people go to see it.

Visiting the House

Today, you can visit this special place. You can see how beautiful and special the house is. You can see the waterfalls the house is built on and the stairs that go into the water.

Think And Write

1. **Scientific Thinking** Why was Fallingwater hard to build?

2. **Scientific Thinking** Why might taking care of the house be hard?

Project — Temperature Watch

Materials

- outdoor thermometer
- paper
- colored pencils

	MORNING	EVENING	WEATHER
SUNDAY			
MONDAY	62	80	
TUESDAY	64	82	
WEDNESDAY			
THURSDAY			
FRIDAY			
SATURDAY			

Procedure

1. Each day for five days, observe the temperature in the morning and in the evening.

2. Record your data in a chart. Draw a picture of the weather that goes with the temperature you recorded.

3. Compare your findings. Which days had the same weather? Which day was the coldest? Was it colder in the morning or in the evening?

Draw Conclusions

1. Why did the weather change each day?

2. What do you think caused the temperature to change from the morning to the evening?

Our Earth

UNIT
C
EARTH SCIENCE

Unit Inquiry

Plants and Erosion

As you do this unit, you will find out about Earth. Plan and do a test. See how plants change the way soil is washed away by water.

Exploring Earth's Surface

Earth's surface is made up of many different materials and can change over time.

Essential Questions

Lesson 1

What Changes Earth's Surface?

Lesson 2

What Are Rocks, Sand, and Soil?

Lesson 3

What Can We Learn from Fossils?

Student eBook
www.hspscience.com

What do YOU wonder?

Why do some rocks have such odd shapes? How does this connect to the Big Idea?

Sandstone Arch in Valley of Fire, Nevada

Essential Question

What Changes Earth's Surface?

Investigate to find out how land shapes can change.

Read and Learn about changes to Earth's surface.

Fast Fact

Changing Landforms

The shape of the Vermilion Cliffs, in Arizona, does not stay the same. Wind and rain wear down the rock and change its shape. You can observe cliffs and other landforms to learn how they change.

Vermilion Cliffs

Weathering is a kind of change that happens when wind and water break down rock into smaller pieces. (p. 200)

Erosion is a kind of change that happens when wind and water move sand and small rocks to a new place. (p. 201)

An **earthquake** is a shaking of Earth's surface that can cause land to rise or fall. (p. 202)

A **volcano** is a place where hot, melted rock called lava comes out of the ground onto Earth's surface. (p. 203)

197

How Land Shapes Change

Ask a Question

How did this river change the land around it?
Investigate to find out. Then read and learn to find out more.

Get Ready

Inquiry Skill Tip

You can use a hand lens to more closely observe changes in small objects.

You need

rock salt

hand lens

forceps and spoon

jar, sand, and water

198

What to Do

Step 1

Hold a grain of rock salt with forceps. **Observe** the size and shape of rock salt with a hand lens.

Step 2

Put a layer of the rock salt in a jar. Add a layer of sand and a few spoonfuls of water. Shake the jar for five minutes.

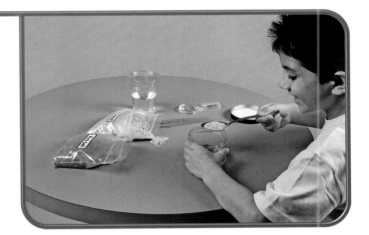

Step 3

Use forceps to remove the rock salt. **Observe**.

Draw Conclusions

How has the rock salt changed?

Independent Inquiry

When you **observe**, you can see how things change. Observe how rocks change.

CAUSE AND EFFECT
Look for the causes and effects of changes to Earth's surface.

Weathering and Erosion

Earth is made up of rock. Often the rock is under water or soil. This rock is Earth's crust. Earth's crust is always changing. One kind of change is caused by weathering. **Weathering** happens when wind and water break down rock into smaller pieces.

Weathering can happen when water freezes in the cracks of rocks. When the water freezes, it takes up more space. It makes the cracks bigger. It can break the rock into pieces.

Strong winds can blow away dry, loose soil and small rocks or sand.

Wind and water may cause erosion. **Erosion** happens when wind or moving water moves sand and small rocks, or pebbles. This movement can cause more weathering and erosion. It changes the shapes of rocks.

Focus Skill **CAUSE AND EFFECT** What are the effects of weathering and erosion?

Water can change the shape of rocks. It can make sharp edges smooth.

The rushing waters of a river wore away rock and formed this canyon.

Earthquakes and Volcanoes

Earthquakes and volcanoes can change Earth's surface quickly.

An **earthquake** is a shaking of Earth's surface. It can cause land to fall or rise. An earthquake may form lakes or cause mudslides. If an earthquake happens in the ocean, it can cause a huge wave to form.

volcano

An earthquake caused this change to Earth's surface.

A **volcano** is a place where hot, melted rock called lava comes out of the ground onto Earth's surface. The lava builds up to form a mountain.

(Focus Skill) CAUSE AND EFFECT

What are some of the effects of earthquakes and volcanoes?

Make a Model

Use clay of different colors to make a model of a volcano. Use your model to tell about volcanoes.

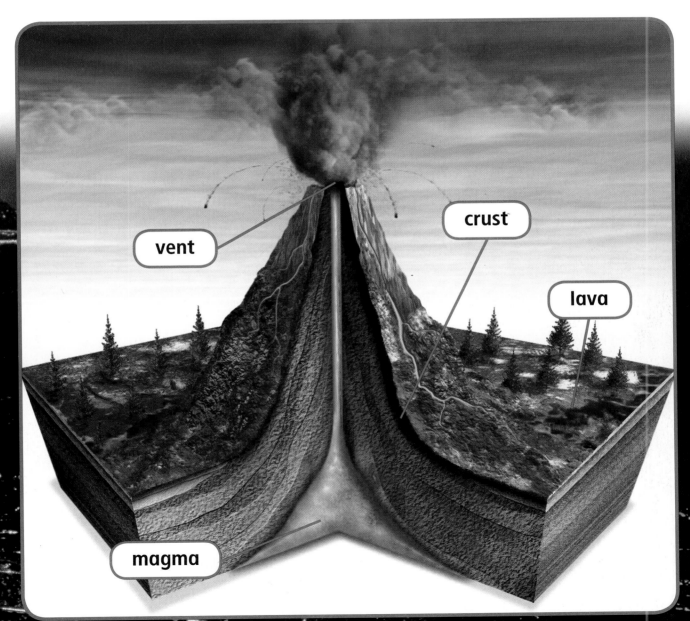

vent

crust

lava

magma

Landforms

Earth's surface has many kinds of landforms. Each kind has a different shape. Some are tall, and some are flat. Each one formed in a different way.

CAUSE AND EFFECT

What can cause islands to form?

A bay is part of an ocean or a lake. It forms when the water covers a low place on the shore.

A delta is a flat triangle of land that may form where a river meets a larger body of water.

Mountains are tall landforms that can form when the plates, or parts, of Earth's crust push against each other.

An island is land that has water all around it. Lava from volcanoes under the oceans can form islands.

Essential Question

What changes Earth's surface?

In this lesson, you learned about changes that can happen to Earth's surface and what causes some of those changes.

1. 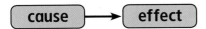 **CAUSE AND EFFECT**
Make a chart like this one. Show the effects that an earthquake and a volcano have on Earth.

cause ⟶ effect

2. VOCABULARY Use the terms **weathering** and **erosion** to tell about this picture.

3. DRAW CONCLUSIONS If you put a rough rock into a river, how will it change over time?

4. SUMMARIZE Write a summary of this lesson. Begin with the sentence **Earth's surface changes.**

Test Prep

5. What happens when water or wind moves sand or small pieces of rock?

   A earthquakes

   B erosion

   C Islands form.

   D Volcanoes form.

Make Connections

 Writing

Description of a Change
Find a picture in this lesson that shows how Earth is changing. Write a few sentences about the picture. Ask a classmate to read the sentences and find the picture you wrote about.

A volcano

Investigate to find out about the hardness of minerals.

Read and Learn about rocks, sand, and soil.

What Are Rocks, Sand, and Soil?

Fast Fact

Sand and Rocks
Tiny grains of sand were once part of large rocks. You can use what you know to draw conclusions about how this change happened.

island in the Indian Ocean

A **boulder** is a very large rock. (p. 210)

A **mineral** is solid matter that is found in nature and that was never living. Most rocks are made of many different minerals. (p. 211)

Soil is bits of rocks mixed with matter that once was living. (p. 212)

207

Hardness of Minerals

Ask a Question

How are these rocks alike? How are they different? Investigate to find out. Then read and learn to find out more.

Get Ready

Inquiry Skill Tip

You can draw conclusions by using observations and what you already know.

You need

minerals

copper penny

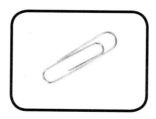

steel paper clip

What to Do

Step ①
Make a hardness chart.

Step ②
Scratch each mineral with your fingernail, a penny, and a paper clip. Record in your chart which objects make a mark on each mineral.

Which Objects Leave Marks on Minerals?

	fingernail	penny	paper clip
mineral 1			
mineral 2			
mineral 3			

Step ③
Objects harder than a mineral leave a mark. Look at your chart and discuss your results.

Draw Conclusions
Draw conclusions about which objects are harder than each mineral.

Independent Inquiry

You can use your observations and what you know to **draw conclusions**. Draw conclusions about the hardness of minerals.

VOCABULARY
boulder
mineral
soil

 **COMPARE AND CONTRAST**
Look for ways rocks are alike and ways they are different.

Rocks and Sand

Rocks are parts of Earth's crust. Some rocks are so large that you can climb them. A **boulder** is a very large rock. Some rocks are so small that you need a microscope to see them. Pebbles and tiny grains of sand are small rocks.

boulder

Rocks are made up of minerals. A **mineral** is solid matter found in nature. A mineral was never living. Not all rocks look and feel the same because rocks are made in different ways and have different minerals. Rocks can have many colors. Some are rough, and some are smooth. Some rocks are harder than others.

sand

 COMPARE AND CONTRAST How are the rocks below alike? How are they different?

limestone

marble

slate

sandstone

granite

obsidian

Soil

Soil is made of small bits of rock mixed with matter that was once living, such as dead plant parts.

There are many kinds of soil. Each kind is made up of different matter, so soils have different properties. A soil may be dark or light. It may feel powdery or sticky. It may have a strong smell.

Some of the things in soil are silt, clay, sand, and humus.

COMPARE AND CONTRAST
How are soils alike? How are they different?

Clay	Silt

Clay is smooth when it is dry. It is sticky when it is wet.	Silt is smooth and powdery.

A Closer Look at Soil
Use a hand lens to look at some soil. What do you see? Work with a classmate to compare observations.

Humus

Humus is brown and soft. It holds water well. Humus includes dead plant parts and other things that were once living.

Sand

Sand grains are rough. They are larger than grains of silt or clay.

Soil for Growing Things

Plants need soil to grow. Soil holds a plant's roots in place. The roots keep the soil from blowing away. A plant's roots take in water and nutrients, or minerals, from the soil. Nutrients help the plant grow and stay healthy.

Soils hold different amounts of water and have different nutrients. Different soils are good for growing different kinds of plants.

 COMPARE AND CONTRAST
How can one soil be better for growing plants than another soil?

Essential Question

What are rocks, sand, and soil?

In this lesson, you learned about different kinds of rocks, sand, and soil and what they can be used for.

1.  **COMPARE AND CONTRAST** Make a chart like this one. Tell how rocks are alike and how they are different.

alike ——— different

2. VOCABULARY Tell how **soil** helps this plant grow.

3. DRAW CONCLUSIONS Why is a soil rich in humus good to use to grow plants?

4. SUMMARIZE Write three sentences that summarize this lesson.

Test Prep

5. Why do different kinds of soil look, smell, and feel different?

Make Connections

 Math

Compare Masses

Choose four rocks. Place two masses on one side of a balance. Place a rock on the other side. Compare the rock's mass to the masses. Which mass is greater? Record the results for each rock.

Investigate to find out about fossils.

Read and Learn about things we can learn from fossils.

Essential Question

What Can We Learn from Fossils?

Fast Fact

Woolly Mammoths

Woolly mammoths lived thousands of years ago. Scientists have found their fossil bones and have put the bones back together. The scientists have communicated what the mammoths looked like. Communicating tells others what we have learned.

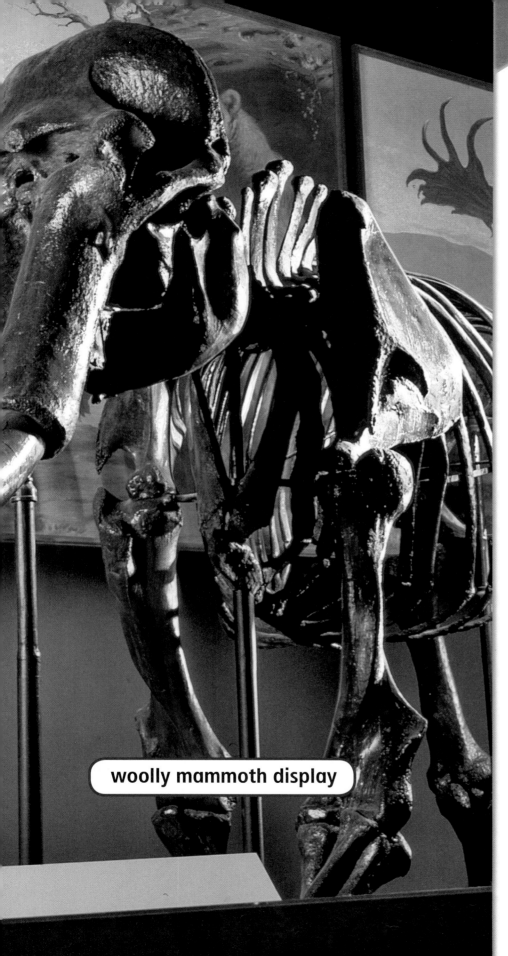

woolly mammoth display

A **dinosaur** is an animal that lived on Earth millions of years ago. Dinosaurs have become extinct. (p. 220)

Extinct is no longer living. Dinosaurs are extinct because there are none living anymore. (p. 220)

A **fossil** is what is left of an animal or plant that lived long ago. A fossil can be a print in a rock or bones that have turned to rock. (p. 220)

Uncovering Fossils

Ask a Question

Why are scientists careful when they dig fossils out of the ground?
Investigate to find out. Then read and learn to find out more.

Get Ready

Inquiry Skill Tip

You can communicate by telling or showing others what you discover.

You need

small objects

clay

tools

What to Do

Step ①

Place a small object inside a flattened ball of clay. Cover the object with clay and let it get hard.

Step ②

Trade clay with a classmate. Use the tools to gently uncover the object in the clay.

Step ③

Communicate to a classmate what you discover.

Draw Conclusions

What can you tell about the object that was in the clay?

Independent Inquiry

You can **communicate** by telling or showing others what you discover. Communicate how you uncovered prints made by objects.

SEQUENCE

Look for the order in which a fossil forms.

Fossils

Dinosaurs were animals that lived millions of years ago on Earth. No dinosaurs live on Earth now. They have all become **extinct**, or have died out. They were not able to survive in their environments.

Scientists have learned about dinosaurs from their fossils. A **fossil** is what is left of an animal or a plant that lived long ago. A fossil can be a footprint or an impression in rock. Fossils can also be shells, teeth, and bones that have turned to rock.

picture of extinct fern

living fern today

fern fossil impression in rock

Scientists compare fossils of plants and animals with plants and animals that live today. This helps the scientists learn about extinct plants and animals.

Fossils can show the sizes of animals. They can give clues about how the animals moved. Fossils may also give clues about where the animals lived and what they ate.

Focus Skill SEQUENCE What happened to some plants and animals of long ago after they died?

Florida panther

fossil of saber-toothed cat

drawing of saber-toothed cat

221

A Trilobite Fossil Forms

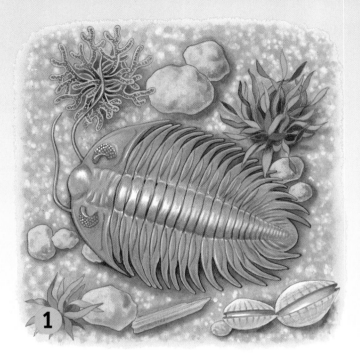

First, a trilobite died. Mud and sand covered the trilobite.

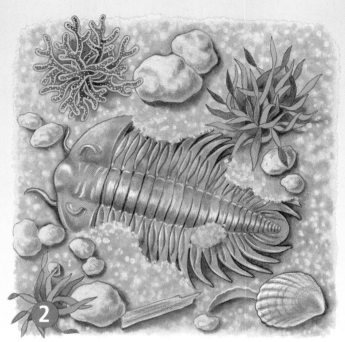

Next, the trilobite's soft parts rotted away. Its shell and other hard parts remained.

How Fossils Form

Fossils form when plants and animals are buried under mud, clay, or sand. The soft parts of the plant or animal rot away. The hard parts turn to rock. The fossils may be found millions of years later.

For more links and animations, go to **www.hspscience.com**

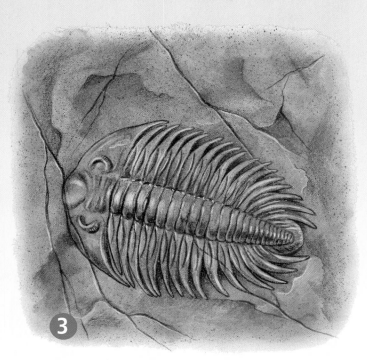

Then, the mud, the sand, and the hard parts of the trilobite slowly turned to rock.

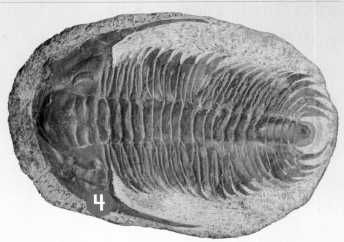

Last, after millions of years, erosion removed the rock covering the fossil, and the fossil was found.

A trilobite was an animal that lived in the sea. A hard outer part covered its soft body. The pictures show how its fossil formed.

Insta-Lab

Make a Print in Clay

Flatten four pieces of clay. Press a different object into each one. Remove the objects. Trade prints with a classmate. Guess what object made each print fossil.

What We Find Out from Fossils

Fossils may be found broken into many pieces. Scientists put the pieces together. They use the fossils to infer what plants and animals of long ago looked like.

Observe each animal and its fossil.

Focus Skill **SEQUENCE** What do scientists do after they find fossil pieces?

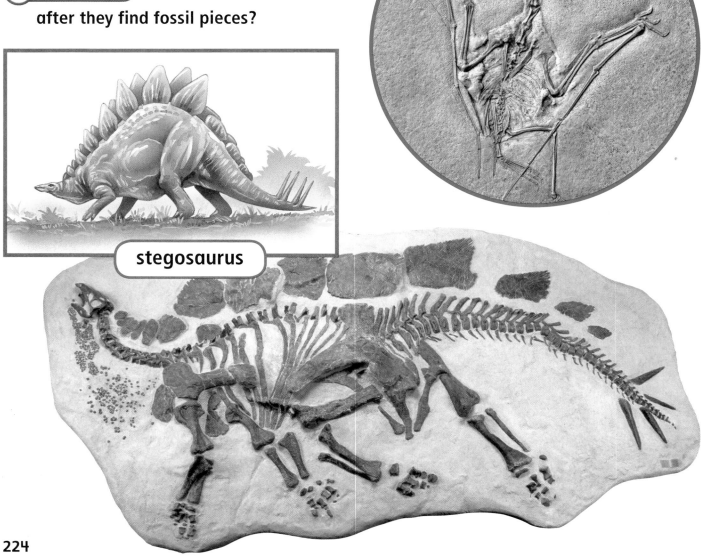

pterodactyl

stegosaurus

Essential Question

What can we learn from fossils?

In this lesson, you learned about fossils, how they are formed, and what we can find out from them.

1.  **SEQUENCE** Make a chart like this one. Show the steps by which a trilobite becomes a fossil.

□ → □ → □

2. VOCABULARY Use the terms **extinct** and **fossil** to tell about this picture.

3. DRAW CONCLUSIONS What can fossils tell us about life in the past?

4. SUMMARIZE Use the vocabulary terms to write a summary of this lesson.

Test Prep

5. Which animal is extinct?

- **A** alligator
- **B** dinosaur
- **C** elephant
- **D** giraffe

Make Connections

 Social Studies

Then and Now
Observe fossils found in your state. Compare them with animals and plants that live today. Draw a picture of a fossil and a picture of a plant or animal that lives today. Tell how they are alike and how they are different.

elephant

mammoth fossil

Marguerite Thomas Williams

Marguerite Thomas Williams spent many years working hard in school. She studied an area of science called geology. Geology is the study of rocks and landforms on Earth.

Dr. Williams was interested in how water changes the shape of Earth. In 1942, Dr. Williams earned a Ph.D. in geology. A Ph.D. is the highest degree a college can give a student. She was the first African American to earn a Ph.D. in geology in the United States.

▶ **DR. MARGUERITE THOMAS WILLIAMS**
▶ Geologist

Think and Write

Why do you think it is important that Williams was the first African American to earn a Ph.D. in geology?

Edward Drinker Cope

▶ **DR. EDWARD DRINKER COPE**

▶ Paleontologist
▶ Told about 1,000 or more kinds of animals from long ago

Edward Drinker Cope was a famous paleontologist, a scientist who studies fossils. Dr. Cope found fossils in several states.

When Dr. Cope began his work, scientists knew about only 18 kinds of dinosaurs. Dr. Cope found bones from 56 kinds of dinosaurs and many other animals of long ago.

Dr. Cope wrote about his work. Other scientists learned from what he had done.

 Think and Write

Why is it important for scientists to share information about their work?

Edward Drinker Cope was the first to find bones from the *Camarasaurus*.

Review and Test Prep

Vocabulary Review

Match each term with the picture that shows its meaning. The page numbers tell you where to look if you need help.

volcano p. 203   **soil** p. 212

boulder p. 210   **fossil** p. 220

1. _____

2. _____

3. _____

4. _____

Check Understanding

5. Write **first**, **next**, and **then** to show the sequence.

 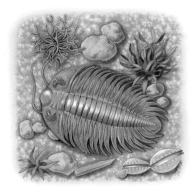 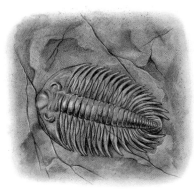

6. Which two things can change Earth's surface quickly?

   A boulders and soil

   B dinosaurs and fossils

   C earthquakes and volcanoes

   D weathering and erosion

Critical Thinking

The Big Idea

7. Tell how these rocks show the effects of erosion.

8. What can fossils tell about animals that lived long ago?

Earth has many natural resources that people use. It is important to protect them to make them last.

Student eBook
www.hspscience.com

What do YOU wonder?

Think about the **Big Idea**. What natural resources do you see in this picture? How can they be used?

Investigate to find out about some of the ways people use water.

Read and Learn about how people can use natural resources.

Essential Question

How Can People Use Natural Resources?

Fast Fact

Water Uses

Rain does not always provide enough water to grow the food people need. Sometimes farmers have to water their crops. You can draw conclusions to find out how people use water the most.

A **resource** is anything people can use to meet their needs. (p. 236)

A **natural resource** is anything in nature people can use to meet their needs. (p. 236)

233

Ways We Use Water

Guided Inquiry

Ask a Question

Why do you think farmers use sprinklers to water their crops? Investigate to find out. Then read and learn to find out more.

Inquiry Skill Tip

To draw conclusions about something, you use your observations and what you know.

You need

paper and pencil

What to Do

Step ①

List the ways you and your classmates use water in one day.

Step ②

Record the data in a chart like this one. Make a mark each time someone uses water.

Ways Our Class Uses Water in One Day

way	times
washing hands	

Step ③

Count the marks at the end of the day.

Draw Conclusions

In what way did your class use water most often?

Independent Inquiry

Draw conclusions about how you use water at home in one day.

Air and Water

Air and water are natural resources. A **resource** is anything that people can use to meet their needs. A **natural resource** is a resource that comes from nature.

People breathe air. They use moving air, or wind, as a source of energy. When wind pushes on a boat's sails, the boat moves across the water.

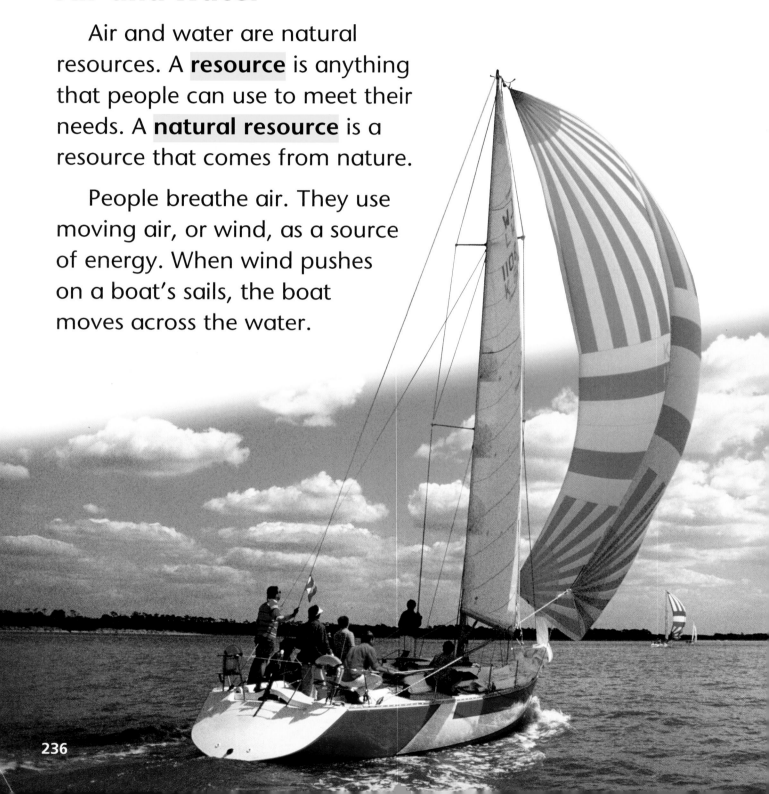

Swimmers can breathe air through a tube called a snorkel.

People use water in many ways. They drink it and use it to bathe, cook, and clean. They use it to grow plants and raise animals. People also enjoy doing water activities for fun.

People travel and ship goods over water in boats. They also use moving water as a source of energy to help them produce electricity.

 MAIN IDEA AND DETAILS
How do people use air and water?

Rocks and Soil

Rocks and soil are two important natural resources. Rocks are pieces of Earth's crust. People use them to make things such as buildings and roads.

People get metals, such as copper, from rocks called ores. Ores may be found near Earth's surface or deep below ground. People dig out an ore and then get the metal out of it. Metal is used to make things such as pots, bikes, and cars.

copper ore

copper pots

copper mine

Soil helps strawberry plants grow.

laying clay bricks

People use soil to grow plants. Soil holds plants in place. It also has nutrients and water that plants need to grow.

Clay is made up of tiny bits of rock. People use clay for building. The clay is formed into bricks or blocks. The clay blocks are dried until they are hard. Then they are used to make buildings and other things.

Focus Skill MAIN IDEA AND DETAILS

How do people use rocks and soil?

Plants

Plants are another important natural resource. People use plants to make and build things. They use cotton to make cloth. They use wood from trees to build houses and to make furniture and paper.

People also use plants for fuel. They may burn tree branches or logs cut from trees. Burning dried plants releases heat energy stored in the plants.

cotton plant

cotton shirt and socks

wooden bookshelves, floor, and chair

Plants from an herb garden are used in cooking.

People also use plants for food. They eat some plant parts. They use other plant parts to make foods such as bread.

 MAIN IDEA AND DETAILS

How do people use plants?

Make a List

Which things in your classroom are made from natural resources? Make a list. Then share it with a classmate. Tell what natural resources were used to make each thing.

Animals

Some people use animals to meet their needs for food and clothing. They drink milk from cows or use it to make foods such as cheese. They eat eggs from chickens and use wool from sheep to make warm clothes.

Focus Skill **MAIN IDEA AND DETAILS**

How do some people use animals?

Essential Question

How can people use natural resources?

In this lesson, you learned about the ways people use natural resources.

1. 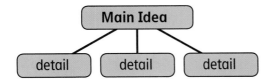 **MAIN IDEA AND DETAILS**
Make a chart like this one. Fill in details about this main idea. **People use natural resources to meet their needs.**

2. VOCABULARY Use the term **natural resources** to tell about this picture.

3. DRAW CONCLUSIONS What are some natural resources you might use if you were working on an art project?

4. SUMMARIZE Use the chart to write a lesson summary.

Test Prep

5. Which natural resource is used for fuel?

   A plants

   B rocks

   C soil

   D water

Make Connections

 Writing

Facts About a Natural Resource

Draw and label a picture of a plant from your state. Then write a few facts about how people use it. Share your facts with classmates.

The mangrove tree grows in salty water.

Investigate to find out about what happens to pollution.

Read and Learn about how people can harm natural resources.

LESSON 2

Essential Question

How Can People Harm Natural Resources?

Fast Fact

Observing Pollution
Litter may harm birds and fish that try to eat it. You can observe pollution to find out what happens to some of it.

Pollution is waste that harms the air, water, or land. (p. 248)

What Happens to Pollution

Guided Inquiry

Ask a Question

Suppose this garbage was found around your school. What should you do with it? What would happen if it were left outside on the ground? Investigate to find out. Then read and learn to find out more.

Get Ready

Inquiry Skill Tip

You can observe things to see how they change over time.

You need

shoe box filled with soil

trash objects

trowel or shovel

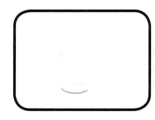

water

What to Do

Step 1

Use a trowel or shovel to put soil in a box. Add trash and more soil. Put the box in a sunny place. Wash your hands if you touch the soil.

Step 2

Water the soil three times each week for one month. At the end of each week, uncover the objects and record what you **observe**.

Step 3

Communicate to your classmates what you observe each week.

Draw Conclusions

Do some of the objects look different than the other objects in the box? Why do you think that is?

Independent Inquiry

You can **observe** things to see how they change over time. Observe what happens to grass and plants covered by trash.

247

VOCABULARY
pollution

CAUSE AND EFFECT
Look for the causes and effects of pollution.

Pollution

Waste that harms air, water, or land is called **pollution**. When people make pollution, they harm natural resources.

Smoke and fumes from factories and cars cause air pollution. Dirty air can harm your lungs and make it hard for you to breathe. It harms plants and animals, too.

Trash, oil spills, and waste from factories cause water pollution. Dirty water can make people and animals ill. It can also harm plants.

Water can become polluted.

Car fumes are one kind of air pollution.

DANGER BEACH CLOSED

248

landfill

Trash that people do not put in trash cans is called litter. Litter can harm plants and animals. Plants covered by litter can not get the light they need to make food. Animals can get trapped by litter. If animals eat litter, they may get sick.

If trash is not placed in a trash can, it becomes litter.

When people put trash in trash cans, it can be taken to landfills. Putting trash in landfills keeps it from making water and land polluted.

Focus Skill **CAUSE AND EFFECT**

What are some effects of air and water pollution?

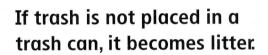

Model an Oil Spill

Put some water in a jar, and add a little oil. Dip a real feather or a paper feather into the oily water. Then feel the feather. How do you think oil spills harm birds?

Wasting Resources

When people use natural resources that they do not need, they waste the resources. Sometimes people want to use land on which trees are growing. They cut all the trees down. They can then use the land, but the trees are wasted.

Building

People need buildings, but they also need to protect natural resources. They may need to cut down some trees to make space for buildings. However, they should not cut down all the trees.

Animals use trees for homes and for food. When trees are cut down, animals must find new homes and new ways to get food. If they cannot do these things, they will die.

 **CAUSE AND EFFECT**

What can cause an animal to need a new home?

People Can Avoid Wasting

People waste resources when they do not turn off water or lights when they are not using them. They also waste resources by throwing away things that can be made into new things. What resources are being wasted in these photographs?

For more links and animations, go to **www.hspscience.com**

Essential Question

How can people harm natural resources?

In this lesson, you learned about how people can harm natural resources through pollution, wasting, and littering.

1.  **CAUSE AND EFFECT**
Make a chart like this one. Show the effects that pollution has on Earth.

cause ⟶ effect

2. VOCABULARY Tell how **pollution** can harm people, plants, and animals.

3. DRAW CONCLUSIONS Why is it important not to waste natural resources?

4. SUMMARIZE Write three sentences that tell what this lesson is mostly about.

Test Prep

5. How do some people protect resources?

Make Connections

 Math

Make a Bar Graph
Ask ten people a question about saving water. For example, "How often do you turn off the water while you brush your teeth?" Show the answers in a bar graph.

How Often Do You Turn Off the Water While You Brush Your Teeth?

number of times

always
sometimes
never

0 1 2 3 4 5 6 7
people

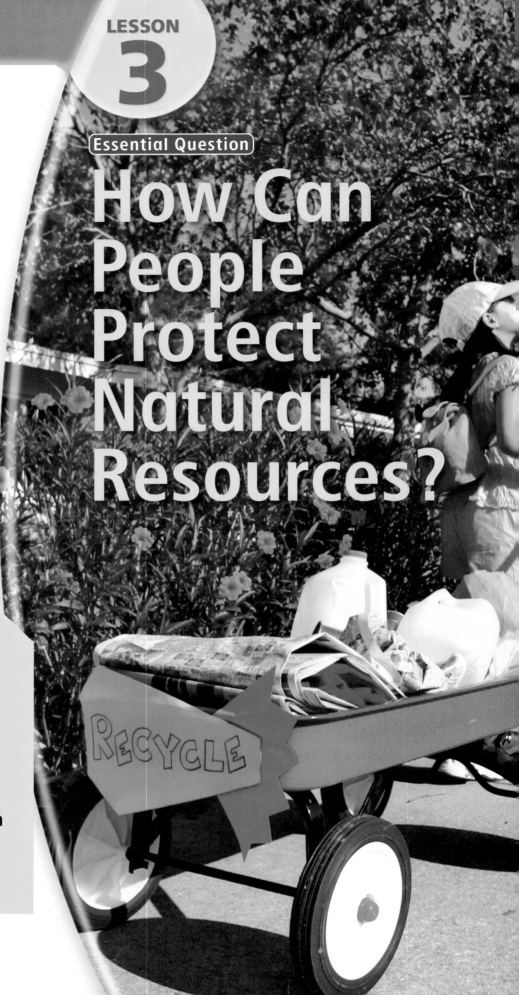

Essential Question

How Can People Protect Natural Resources?

Investigate to find out how you can reuse things.

Read and Learn about how people can protect natural resources.

Fast Fact

Recycle Things
Paper, bottles, and even playground equipment can be made from old materials. You can plan an investigation to find out how to use things in new ways.

To **reuse** is to use a resource again. (p. 258)

To **reduce** is to use less of a resource. (p. 258)

To **recycle** is to use the materials in old things to make new things. (p. 259)

Endangered is in danger of not being alive anymore. People can help endangered animals by protecting the places they live. (p. 261)

255

How to Reuse Things

Guided Inquiry

Ask a Question

What was this pencil holder made from? How does that help Earth?

Investigate to find out. Then read and learn to find out more.

Get Ready

Inquiry Skill Tip

When you plan an investigation, you ask a question and find a way to answer it.

You need

used things

colored markers

glue

newspaper

What to Do

Step 1

How can you make something useful from used things? **Plan an investigation** to find out.

Step 2

Write the steps you need to take.

Step 3

Follow your steps to make a useful object. Then communicate to classmates how you made your object.

Draw Conclusions

Is there another way you could use the materials?

Independent Inquiry

When you **plan an investigation**, you ask a question and find a way to answer the question. Plan an investigation about making an instrument from used things.

VOCABULARY
reuse
reduce
recycle
endangered

 **CAUSE AND EFFECT**
Look for the effects of protecting natural resources.

Reuse, Reduce, and Recycle

People protect natural resources when they use less of them. One way to do this is to **reuse** things, or use them again. When you reuse things, you need fewer new things made from natural resources. You make less trash, too.

You save natural resources when you **reduce**, or lessen, the amount you use. Walking or riding a bike reduces the amount of gas that is used. It also keeps the air cleaner.

Reusing a lunchbox makes less trash and saves resources.

This woman is saving gasoline by not driving her car.

recycling

Recycling is another way to save natural resources. When people **recycle**, they use the materials in old things to make new things. This makes less trash, too. Some things made of glass, plastic, metal, and paper can be recycled. What things do you recycle?

Focus Skill CAUSE AND EFFECT
What happens when people reuse things?

Reuse a Plastic Jar
How many ways can you and your classmates think of to reuse a plastic jar? Write your ideas on slips of paper, and put the slips in the jar. Then take turns reading the ideas.

Conserving

Most people use coal, gas, and oil for energy. In time, these natural resources will be used up. People must conserve them, or use them wisely to make them last longer. Using other energy sources can help.

Some people use the power of water and wind to produce electricity. Some use the energy of sunlight. Water, wind, and sunlight do not get used up as coal, gas, and oil do.

dam

windmills

This park helps keep
endangered animals safe.

In places where many trees are cut
down, people can plant new trees. Trees
provide homes for animals, and the roots
hold the soil in place.

Some kinds of animals are **endangered**.
This means that very few of these animals
are left. If people do not protect them, they
may all die. People can help by making sure
the animals' homes are safe. They can also
move the animals to places where they can
get the things they need to live.

(Focus Skill) **CAUSE AND EFFECT** What will happen to some
natural resources in time if people keep using them?

Reducing Pollution

Cities and towns can reduce pollution by passing laws that protect natural resources. In many places, littering and burning trash are against the law. Companies must follow the laws, too. They may not dump harmful waste into water or onto the ground. Factories must reduce the amount of smoke and gases they make. This keeps the air cleaner.

These children are reducing pollution at their school by picking up litter. How can you help reduce pollution?

 **CAUSE AND EFFECT** What are the effects of laws that protect natural resources?

Essential Question

How can people protect natural resources?

In this lesson, you learned that people can protect natural resources by reusing, reducing, and recycling.

1. 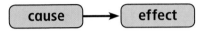 **CAUSE AND EFFECT**
Make a chart like this one. Show the effects of recycling in your community.

cause ⟶ effect

2. VOCABULARY Tell how people can help endangered animals.

3. DRAW CONCLUSIONS What could you do if you saw a natural resource, such as water, being wasted?

4. SUMMARIZE Write a lesson summary. Begin with the sentence **People can protect natural resources**.

Test Prep

5. How do people reduce pollution?

    A They cut down trees.

    B They make more litter.

    C They use less gasoline.

    D They burn trash.

Make Connections

 Art

Poster

Make a poster to show some useful things you can make with an empty milk carton. Label each new thing you can make.

Wild Waves

Cortes Bank is a great place to surf. But this area is different from other surfing spots. Cortes Bank is about 100 miles from land!

Ridge Makes Rough Waters

Cortes Bank is an undersea mountain range that is, in some places, only three feet below the surface. It has some of the biggest waves in the world.

264

Predicting Waves

Ocean experts use different tools to measure ocean waves. They use information from satellites in space and weather maps. The information is then put into a computer, which can predict how fast and how high waves will be.

 Think and Write

Why do you think surfers like to surf at Cortes Bank?

Surf's Up

According to experts, waves at Cortes Bank can reach more than 70 feet high. That's as tall as a seven-story building! Some waves move at speeds of more than 50 kilometers (30 miles) per hour.

Seven Story Tall Building

 Find out more. Log on to
www.hspscience.com

Vocabulary Review

Use the terms below to complete the sentences. The page numbers tell you where to look if you need help.

resource p. 236   **reuse** p. 258

natural resource p. 236   **recycle** p. 259

pollution p. 248   **endangered** p. 261

1. When very few animals of a certain kind are left, that kind of animal is _____.

2. When you use old things to make new things, you _____.

3. A resource that comes from nature is a _____.

4. When you use things again, you _____ them.

5. Anything people can use to meet their needs is a _____.

6. Waste that harms air, water, or land is _____.

Check Understanding

7. How can people harm natural resources?

    A They can waste them.

    B They can protect them.

    C They can reuse them.

    D They can save them.

8. Which tells an effect of recycling?

(Focus Skill)

    F It makes more trash.

    G It makes more pollution.

    H It saves natural resources.

    J It wastes natural resources.

Critical Thinking

9. What natural resources do you need to grow a plant?

10. How can you conserve natural resources at home?  The **Big Idea**

Visual Summary

Tell how each picture shows the **Big Idea** for its chapter.

Big Idea

Earth's surface is made up of many different materials and can change over time.

Big Idea

Earth has many natural resources that people use. It is important to protect them to make them last.

UNIT
D
EARTH SCIENCE

Weather and Space

Unit Inquiry

Evaporation

As you do this unit, you will learn about weather and space. Plan and do a test. Form three different puddles. See which one evaporates first.

CHAPTER 7 Weather

What's the Big Idea?

Weather can be observed, measured, predicted, and compared.

Essential Questions

Lesson 1
How Does Weather Change?

Lesson 2
Why Do We Measure Weather?

Lesson 3
What Is the Water Cycle?

Go online
Student eBook
www.hspscience.com

270

What do YOU wonder?

How do people know what the weather is going to be like? Think about the **Big Idea** to help you answer.

Investigate to find out about changes in weather.

Read and Learn about how weather changes.

Essential Question

How Does Weather Change?

Fast Fact

Rainbows
It takes both light and water to make a rainbow. You may see a rainbow if the sun shines during or right after a rain shower. By observing the weather, you can see its patterns.

Weather is what the air outside is like. The weather in summer is often sunny and hot. (p. 276)

A **weather pattern** is a change in the weather that repeats. (p. 276)

A **season** is a time of year that has a certain kind of weather. The four seasons are spring, summer, fall, and winter. (p. 277)

Changes in Weather

Ask a Question

What kind of weather is causing the branches to move? Investigate to find out. Then read and learn to find out more.

Get Ready

Inquiry Skill Tip

When you observe weather, you see how it changes. You also see weather patterns.

You need

poster board and markers

What to Do

Step ①

Make up a symbol to stand for each kind of weather. Then draw a chart like this one.

Weather

Monday	
Tuesday	
Wednesday	
Thursday	
Friday	

Step ②

Observe the weather each day for 5 days. Record what you **observed**.

Step ③

What kinds of weather did you **observe**? Share your information.

Draw Conclusions

Can the weather change more than once a day?

Independent Inquiry

When you **observe**, you can see how things change. Observe the weather two times each day for five days. Tell what you observe.

VOCABULARY

weather
weather pattern
season

 **SEQUENCE**

Look for the order of seasons and the ways the weather changes from one season to the next.

Weather

What is the weather like today? Is it hot or cold? Is it rainy, snowy, sunny, cloudy, or windy? **Weather** is what the air outside is like. It can change in just a few hours or over many months. A change in the weather that repeats is called a **weather pattern**.

 **SEQUENCE**   **What usually happens after it rains?**

Spring

A **season** is a time of year that has a certain kind of weather. In many places, the weather changes with each season. In spring, the air gets warmer. In some places, it is very rainy in spring. As the weather gets warmer and wetter, plants begin to grow.

Focus Skill SEQUENCE How does the air change in spring?

Insta-Lab

Model a Rainbow

Place a mirror in a jar of water. Make the room dark. Shine a flashlight on the mirror. Move the light around. Shine it from different directions until you see rainbow colors.

Summer

Summer comes after spring. In most places, summer is the warmest time of year. The days are often hot and sunny. But storms can quickly change the weather. In summer, trees and other plants have a lot of leaves.

Focus Skill **SEQUENCE** Which season comes before summer?

Fall

Fall is the next season. In fall, the air gets cooler. Some fall days are sunny, while others are cloudy. In fall, the leaves of some trees change color and then drop off. Some plants stop growing and die.

Focus Skill **SEQUENCE** How may trees change from summer to fall?

Winter

After fall, winter comes. This is the coldest season. In some places, it gets cold enough to snow. In these places, many trees and bushes have no leaves until spring.

In other places, the air cools down just a little. It may never snow there. Many trees and plants keep their leaves. Many flowers keep growing.

Spring comes again after winter. The pattern of changing seasons goes on.

Focus Skill **SEQUENCE** **What might happen to trees when winter ends?**

Essential Question

How does weather change?

In this lesson, you learned about changes in weather and about the seasons.

1.  **SEQUENCE**
Make a chart like this one. Show the sequence of the seasons.

2. VOCABULARY Describe how **weather patterns** change from summer to fall.

3. DRAW CONCLUSIONS What might happen if winter weather went on longer than usual?

4. SUMMARIZE Write a summary of the lesson. Begin with the sentence **Weather can change with the seasons.**

Test Prep

5. How can you tell it is spring?
A Trees have no leaves.
B Trees grow new leaves.
C Some leaves change color.
D Trees have lots of leaves.

Make Connections

 Writing

Weather Report
Choose a season. Write a short weather report for one day of that season where you live. Then present your weather report to the class. Use a map to point out your state.

Investigate to
find out how
to measure
temperature.

Read and Learn
about why people
measure weather.

Essential Question

Why Do We Measure Weather?

Fast Fact

Changes in Weather

The coldest
temperature ever
measured in the
United States was
recorded in Alaska
on January 23, 1971.
You can compare
temperatures to see
how the weather
changes.

Computers help
measure weather.

Temperature is a measure of how hot or cold something is. (p. 287)

A **thermometer** is a tool that measures an object's temperature. (p. 287)

Wind is air that is moving. (p. 288)

Precipitation is water that falls from the sky. Rain, snow, sleet, and hail are kinds of precipitation. (p. 290)

Measure Temperature

Ask a Question

How can this child decide what kind of clothing to wear? Investigate to find out. Then read and learn to find out more.

Get Ready

Inquiry Skill Tip

When you compare temperatures, you can see patterns in the way temperatures change.

You need

thermometer

What to Do

Step ①

Make a chart like this one.

<table>
<tr><th colspan="2">Temperature</th></tr>
<tr><td>Morning</td><td></td></tr>
<tr><td>Noon</td><td></td></tr>
<tr><td>Late Afternoon</td><td></td></tr>
</table>

Step ②

Read the thermometer in the morning, at noon, and in the late afternoon. Record each temperature.

Step ③

Compare the temperatures.

Draw Conclusions

Which time of day had the highest temperature? Why do you think that was?

Independent Inquiry

When you **compare** temperatures over time you look for a pattern of change. Compare temperatures over three days to see if there is a pattern.

VOCABULARY
temperature
thermometer
wind
precipitation

 MAIN IDEA AND DETAILS

Look for details that tell why and how weather is measured.

Measuring Weather

Scientists use tools to measure the weather. Some tools tell how warm the air is. Others tell how fast the wind is blowing. Still others tell how much rain has fallen.

Measuring weather helps scientists see patterns. Patterns help the scientists predict the weather. Then they can warn people when a big storm is coming.

 MAIN IDEA AND DETAILS

What parts of weather do scientists measure?

Measuring Temperature

A tool called a **thermometer** measures **temperature**, or how warm something is. Scientists use thermometers to record the temperature of the air. In some thermometers, warmer air makes the liquid in the thermometer go up. Cooler air makes the liquid go down.

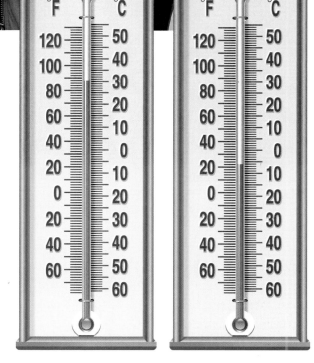

Which thermometer shows the temperature on a cold day?

 **MAIN IDEA AND DETAILS**

How can you use a thermometer to learn about the weather?

Measuring Wind

Wind is moving air. It can move in different directions. Scientists use a weather vane to find out which way the wind is blowing. The wind turns the arrow on the vane. The arrow points to the direction the wind is coming from.

Draw and Compare

Look outside. Is the wind blowing? How can you tell? Draw a picture that shows what the wind is doing. Use your picture to tell about the wind's speed.

Scientists measure the speed of wind with a tool called an anemometer.

You can use the pictures on this page to estimate wind speed. They show the effects of wind at different speeds. The wind speeds are measured in miles per hour.

anemometer

 **MAIN IDEA AND DETAILS**
What tools measure wind? What do they help you learn?

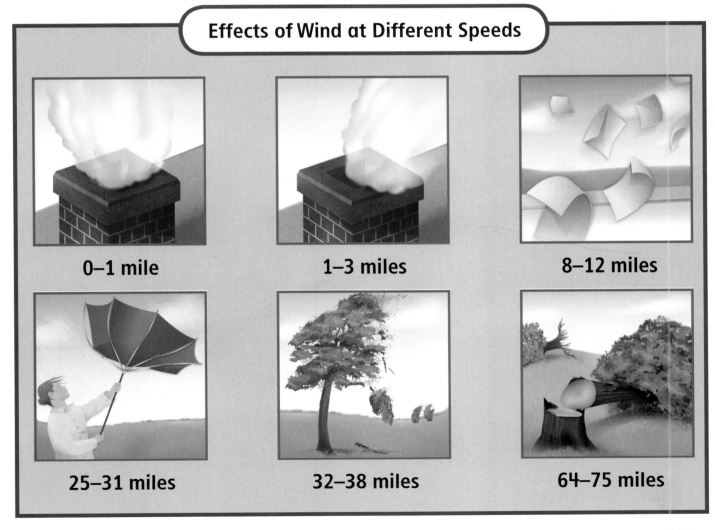

Effects of Wind at Different Speeds

0–1 mile

1–3 miles

8–12 miles

25–31 miles

32–38 miles

64–75 miles

Measuring Precipitation

Water that falls from the sky is called **precipitation**. Rain, snow, sleet, and hail are kinds of precipitation.

Scientists use a rain gauge to find out how much rain falls. This container catches rain. Then scientists can measure how many inches of rain fell. You can use a ruler and a jar to make your own rain gauge.

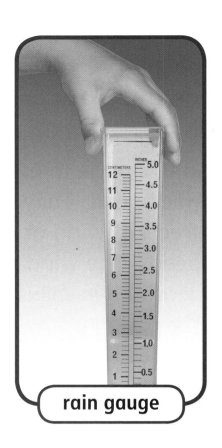

rain gauge

 MAIN IDEA AND DETAILS

What is precipitation? Name some kinds of precipitation.

Essential Question

Why do we measure weather?

In this lesson, you learned why people measure weather.

1. 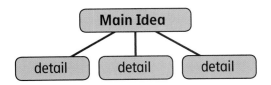 **MAIN IDEA AND DETAILS**
Make a chart like this one.
Fill in details about this main
idea. **Scientists use tools to
measure weather.**

2. VOCABULARY Use the term
precipitation to tell about
this picture.

3. DRAW CONCLUSIONS Why
is it important to measure
weather?

4. SUMMARIZE Write sentences
to tell what this lesson is
mostly about. Begin with how
measuring the weather helps
people.

Test Prep

5. How do scientists learn about
weather?

Make Connections

 Math

Make a Bar Graph
Rainfall changes from month
to month. This chart shows the
rainfall in Tucson, Arizona, for four
months. Use the data to make a
bar graph. What can you tell from
your graph?

Tucson, Arizona

Month	Rainfall
March	2 inches
July	3 inches
September	4 inches
October	2 inches

Investigate to find out about water in the air.

Read and Learn about what the water cycle is.

What Is the Water Cycle?

Fast Fact

Water Everywhere

Water is in lakes, rivers, and oceans. It is also in the air. You know that water falls from the air into bodies of water. Now you will infer how water gets into the air.

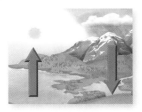

The **water cycle** is the movement of water from Earth's surface into the air and back to Earth's surface. (p. 296)

To **evaporate** is to change from liquid water into a gas. Water evaporates when heat is added. (p. 296)

To **condense** is to change from water vapor gas into liquid water. Water vapor condenses when it is cooled. (p. 296)

A **drought** is a long time when it does not rain. During a drought, the land may become dry, and plants may die. (p. 298)

293

Water in the Air

Guided Inquiry

Ask a Question

Where does the water from a puddle go when the puddle disappears?
Investigate to find out. Then read and learn to find out more.

Get Ready

Inquiry Skill Tip

When you infer, you use what you observe to figure out what happened.

You need

2 zip-top bags

colored water

tape

What to Do

Step ①

Fill each bag halfway with water. Zip the bags closed.

Step ②

Tape one bag to a window in the sun. Tape the other bag to a window in the shade.

Step ③

Wait 30 minutes. Then observe both bags. Record what you observe.

Draw Conclusions

Which bag shows more change? **Infer** what caused the change.

Independent Inquiry

When you **infer**, you use what you see to figure out what happened. Observe two cups of water, one in sun and one in shade. Infer why changes happen.

VOCABULARY
water cycle
evaporate
condense
drought

 **CAUSE AND EFFECT**
Look for causes and effects as you read about the water cycle.

The Water Cycle

Water moves over and over again from Earth's surface into the air and then back to Earth's surface. This movement of water is called the **water cycle**.

Focus Skill CAUSE AND EFFECT
What makes water move from Earth into the air?

Science Up Close

What Happens During the Water Cycle

3 The water vapor cools and **condenses**, or changes into tiny drops of water.

2 The gas, called water vapor, is pushed upward and meets cool air.

1 The sun's heat makes water **evaporate**, or change to a gas.

4 The water droplets join with specks of dust in the air, forming clouds.

5 The water drops join into larger drops. These heavy drops fall as rain or snow.

6 Precipitation flows into streams, lakes, and oceans. Then the water cycle begins again.

For more links and animations, go to **www.hspscience.com**

Droughts

Sometimes it does not rain for a long time. This time is called a **drought**. During a drought, it may be hotter than usual. The land may get very dry. Streams and ponds may dry up. Winds may blow away the soil.

Without water, plants and animals may die. People try to use very little water during a drought.

corn plants harmed by a drought

CAUSE AND EFFECT

What can happen because of a drought?

Floods

If a lot of rain falls, it can cause a flood. Rivers and lakes overflow. Some land is covered with water.

Too much water can kill plants and animals. Homes can be ruined. People must get to safe, dry places during a flood.

Focus Skill **CAUSE AND EFFECT** What can happen because of a flood?

Insta-Lab

Model a Flood

Fill a shallow pan with soil. Shape some hills. Use a bowl of water for a lake. Add small objects to the scene. Sprinkle water until you model a flood. Share your results.

Storms

Storms are a kind of weather that can be harmful. A thunderstorm has rain, thunder, and lightning. The rain from the storm may cause a flood. Lightning may strike trees and other tall things.

When it is cold, a lot of snow may fall. A snowstorm with strong winds is called a blizzard. The blowing snow makes it hard to see. Stay indoors during thunderstorms and snowstorms to keep safe.

CAUSE AND EFFECT

Why are some storms harmful?

Essential Question

What is the water cycle?

In this lesson, you learned about the water cycle, droughts, floods, and storms.

1. **CAUSE AND EFFECT** (Focus Skill)
Make a chart like this one. Show the effects that droughts can have on land.

cause ➔ effect

2. **VOCABULARY** Explain what happens during the **water cycle**.

3. **DRAW CONCLUSIONS** Why do people try to use very little water during a drought?

4. **SUMMARIZE** Use the vocabulary to write three sentences about the lesson.

Test Prep

5. It has not rained for a long time. It is hot, and the soil is dry. What is this time called?

   A a flood

   B a blizzard

   C a drought

   D a thunderstorm

Make Connections

 Art

Water Cycle Poster
Make a poster to show the water cycle. On your poster, label the parts of the water cycle.

The Coldest Place on Earth

Experts say that Antarctica is the coldest place on Earth. If it's so cold, how do animals and people stay warm there?

Cold Weather, Warm Penguins

Penguins are birds that live in Antarctica. They stay warm because they have feathers that are very small and close together. The feathers have oil on them. Cold air and water cannot get through the feathers to touch the penguins' skin.

Weddell seals also live in Antarctica. They swim in the cold ocean water to catch fish and other food. Weddell seals stay warm because they have a layer of blubber, or fat. A coat of thick fur keeps water from touching the seals' skin.

302

Keeping People Warm

Scientists who work in Antarctica have learned how to stay warm as well. When they are outside, scientists wear layers of special clothing. The clothing helps people stay warm the same way animals do. It keeps the cold air from reaching their skin.

 Think and Write

What are some other things people have learned from observing animals?

Playful Penguin Facts

❄ Penguins can waddle faster than humans can walk.

❄ Penguins line up and dive into the water again and again.

❄ Penguins sometimes toboggan, or slide, on their bellies.

❄ Penguins surf waves to get back to shore.

Find out more. Log on to
www.hspscience.com

Vocabulary Review

Use the terms to complete the sentences.
The page numbers tell you where to look
if you need help.

weather pattern p. 276   **precipitation** p. 290

thermometer p. 287   **water cycle** p. 296

1. Rain, snow, and sleet are kinds
of _____.

2. The movement of water from Earth's
surface into the air and back is
the _____.

3. A weather change that repeats is
a _____.

4. One tool that measures the weather is
a _____.

Check Understanding

5. Put these seasons in the
correct sequence.

(Focus Skill)

spring   fall   summer   winter

6. Think about weather patterns. Write about the four seasons. Tell what each season's weather is like.

7. How are these tools alike?

A Both measure rainfall.
B Both measure temperature.
C Both measure weather.
D Both measure wind.

Critical Thinking

8. Think about the water cycle. Explain what will happen to a puddle when the sun shines on it.

9. Write about three tools a scientist uses to learn about a thunderstorm and why it is important to measure weather.

The **Big Idea**

CHAPTER 8

The Solar System

What's the Big Idea?

Earth is a planet. Changes happen on Earth and in the sky from day to night and from season to season.

Essential Questions

Go online Student eBook www.hspscience.com

What do you wonder?

Think about the **Big Idea**.
What seems to happen to the
moon during a month?

307

Investigate to find out about stars and light.

Read and Learn about stars and planets.

Essential Question

What Are Stars and Planets?

Fast Fact

Starry Night
Stars are always in the sky, even during the day. You can infer why we see most stars only at night.

The **solar system** is the sun, its planets, and other objects that move around the sun. (p. 312)

A **planet** is a large ball of rock or gas that moves around the sun. Earth is our planet. (p. 312)

An **orbit** is the path a planet takes as it moves around another object. (p. 313)

A **star** is a big ball of hot gases that gives off light and heat energy. The sun is the closest star to Earth. (p. 314)

A **constellation** is a group of stars that forms a pattern. (p. 314)

Stars and Light

Guided Inquiry

Ask a Question

The sun is a very bright star we can see in the daytime. Why can't we see other stars during the day?
Investigate to find out. Then read and learn to find out more.

Get Ready

You need

black paper and tape

"star" cup

flashlight

What to Do

Step ①

Tape the paper to a wall. Point the bottom of the cup toward the paper. Shine the flashlight into the cup. What do you see?

Step ②

Turn off the lights. Shine the flashlight again. What do you see now?

Step ③

Infer why the "stars" look different with the lights on and with the lights off.

Draw Conclusions

What happens to the "stars" if you shine the flashlight from further away?

Independent Inquiry

When you **infer**, you use what you see to figure out why something happened. Infer why some stars might seem brighter in the night sky than other stars.

VOCABULARY

solar system
planet
orbit
star
constellation

 MAIN IDEA AND DETAILS

Look for details about the solar system.

The Solar System

The **solar system** is made up mainly of the sun, the planets, and the planets' moons. A **planet** is a large ball of rock or gas that moves around the sun. Earth is a planet in the solar system.

You can see a few parts of the solar system at night. During the day, they are still there. You just cannot see them when it is light outside.

Mars

Earth

Venus

Mercury

sun

The sun is the center of the solar system. The planets move in paths around the sun. Each path is called an **orbit**.

The planets are different from one another. They look different. They are different sizes. They are at different distances from the sun, and they move in different orbits around it.

Focus Skill **MAIN IDEA AND DETAILS**
What are the parts of the solar system?

Neptune

Uranus

Saturn

Jupiter

Insta-Lab

Change the Size You See
Find out why large planets look small from Earth. Hold a ball close to your eyes. Then slowly move it away from you. How does the ball's size seem to change? Tell why you think this happens.

Stars

A **star** is a huge ball of hot gases. The hot gases give off light and heat energy. The closest star to Earth is the sun.

You can see the sun in the daytime, but most stars can be seen only at night. Some stars are smaller than the sun. Others are bigger. They all look like tiny points of light because they are so far away. A group of stars that forms a pattern is called a **constellation**.

(Focus Skill) MAIN IDEA AND DETAILS

What is a star?

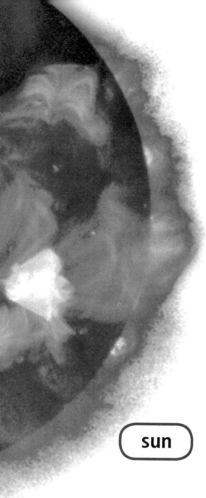

sun

Orion

Big Dipper, part of the constellation Ursa Major

Little Dipper, part of the constellation Ursa Minor

Essential Question

What are stars and planets?

In this lesson, you learned about the solar system and stars.

1. 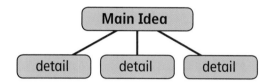 **MAIN IDEA AND DETAILS**
Make a chart like this one. Fill in details about this main idea. **The solar system is made up of the sun, planets, and moons.**

```
        ┌───────────┐
        │ Main Idea │
        └───────────┘
         ╱    │    ╲
   ┌────────┐┌────────┐┌────────┐
   │ detail ││ detail ││ detail │
   └────────┘└────────┘└────────┘
```

2. VOCABULARY Use the terms **constellation** and **star** to tell about this picture.

3. DRAW CONCLUSIONS Why can you see stars only some of the time?

4. SUMMARIZE Write a lesson summary that uses the vocabulary terms.

Test Prep

5. When is the only time you can see most stars?

    A in the morning
    B in the afternoon
    C in the daytime
    D at night

Make Connections

 Writing

Report About a Planet
Choose a planet. Find out four facts about it, and write a short report. Share your report with the class.

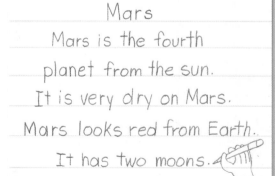

Mars
Mars is the fourth
planet from the sun.
It is very dry on Mars.
Mars looks red from Earth.
It has two moons.

Investigate to find out why shadows change.

Read and Learn about what causes day and night.

What Causes Day and Night?

Fast Fact

Lighting Earth
Most parts of Earth have light and darkness each day because Earth is always spinning. You can observe the effects of Earth's movements.

Vocabulary Preview

To **rotate** is to spin around like a top. Earth rotates one time every 24 hours. (p. 320)

317

Why Shadows Change

Ask a Question

How can you tell what time of day it is in this picture? Investigate to find out. Then read and learn to find out more.

Get Ready

Inquiry Skill Tip

When you observe, you use your senses to learn about things.

You need

two pieces of chalk of different colors

What to Do

Step 1

Stand outside in the morning. Have a partner trace your feet with chalk.

Step 2

Have your partner use chalk of a different color to trace your shadow.

Step 3

Wait two hours. Stand in the same place again. Have your partner trace your shadow again. Repeat two hours later. Communicate what you **observe**.

Draw Conclusions

Did your shadow change position? Why do you think that happened?

Independent Inquiry

When you **observe**, you use your senses to learn about things. Use measurement tools to observe how your shadow changes over time.

319

VOCABULARY
rotate

 **CAUSE AND EFFECT**

Look for the effects of Earth's rotation on day and night and on shadows.

Earth's Rotation

It looks as if the sun rises in one place in the morning and sets in another place at night. The sun does not really move across the sky. Earth is moving.

Earth spins around and around like a top. It takes about 24 hours for Earth to **rotate**, or spin all the way around. One rotation, or spin, of Earth takes one day.

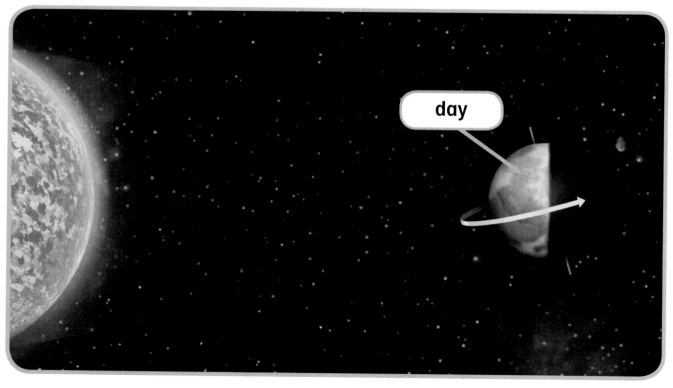

day

Earth's rotation causes day and night. Sunlight shines on only the part of Earth that is facing the sun. This side of Earth has daytime. The other side is dark and has nighttime.

As Earth rotates, the part that was light turns away from the sun and gets dark. The part that was dark moves into the light. In most places, this pattern of day and night repeats every 24 hours.

 CAUSE AND EFFECT

How does Earth's rotation cause day and night?

Model Day and Night

Put a piece of tape on a globe. Slowly spin the globe as you shine a flashlight on it. When is the tape in the light? When is it in the dark?

night

morning

Changes in Shadows

When an object does not allow the sun's light to pass, it makes a shadow. As Earth rotates, the sun seems to move. The sun's light shines on objects from different directions as the day goes on. This causes the positions, sizes, and shapes of shadows to change.

noon

Look at the pictures to see how a shadow changes. When is the shadow long? When is it short? How does the direction the sun shines from change the shadow?

Focus Skill CAUSE AND EFFECT

What causes shadows to change?

afternoon

What causes day and night?

In this lesson, you learned about Earth's rotation and shadows.

1.  **CAUSE AND EFFECT** Make a chart like this one. Show what effects the sun has on Earth.

cause ⟶ effect

2. VOCABULARY Use the term **rotate** to tell why shadows change.

3. DRAW CONCLUSIONS How can you tell when the part of Earth where you live is facing away from the sun?

4. SUMMARIZE Use the chart to tell what this lesson is mostly about. Start with **When Earth faces the sun.**

Test Prep

5. How does Earth's rotation cause day and night?

Make Connections

 Math

Make a Bar Graph

Different planets have different numbers of hours in their days. This is because they all rotate at different speeds. Make a bar graph that shows the number of hours in a day for each planet.

Number of Hours in a Day on Different Planets

planet

Earth
Jupiter
Saturn
Neptune
Mars

0 5 10 15 20 25
number of hours

Investigate to find out why the moon seems to shine.

Read and Learn about how and why the moon seems to change.

Essential Question

Why Does the Moon Seem to Change?

Fast Fact

Moonlight
The light we see from the moon really comes from the sun. You can make a model to show how this happens.

The **moon** is a huge ball of rock that orbits Earth. The moon takes almost one month to go all the way around Earth. (p. 328)

Why the Moon Seems to Shine

Guided Inquiry

Ask a Question

Does the moon always look round? What other shapes can the moon seem to be? Investigate to find out. Then read and learn to find out more.

Get Ready

Inquiry Skill Tip
You can make a model to show how something happens.

You need

foam ball

foil

craft stick

flashlight

What to Do

Step **1**

Work with a partner. Wrap foil around a ball to **make a model** of the moon. Use a craft stick to make a handle.

Step **2**

Hold the handle. Look at the ball in the dark. What does it look like?

Step **3**

Shine the flashlight on the ball. What does it look like now?

Draw Conclusions

What effect did the light have on the ball?

Independent Inquiry

You can **make a model** to show how something happens. Make a model to show how the moon orbits Earth.

VOCABULARY
moon

 **CAUSE AND EFFECT**

Look for the cause of the changes in the way you see the moon.

The Moon Shapes You See

The **moon** is a huge ball of rock that moves in an orbit around Earth. It takes nearly one month for the moon to orbit, or travel around, Earth.

On many nights, the moon seems to shine brightly. But the moon does not give off light of its own, as stars do. It reflects light from the sun.

full moon

first quarter moon

new moon

about 29 days

The moon is always orbiting Earth. So the part you can see of the moon's lit side changes each night. This makes it seem as if the moon's shape changes.

The phases, or shapes you see, change as the moon moves. The changes follow a pattern that repeats about every 29 days.

 **CAUSE AND EFFECT**

What happens because the moon moves around Earth?

last quarter moon

crescent moon

329

Investigate to find out about Earth's tilt.

Read and Learn about what causes the seasons.

Essential Question

What Causes the Seasons?

Fast Fact

Summertime
When North America has summer, South America has winter. You can communicate other facts about the seasons.

A **season** is a time of the year that has a certain kind of weather. The four seasons are spring, summer, fall, and winter. (p. 339)

Earth's Tilt

Ask a Question

What season is it in this picture? How do you know? What causes seasons?

Investigate to find out. Then read and learn to find out more.

Get Ready

Inquiry Skill Tip

When you communicate your ideas, you tell or show others what you know.

You need

foam ball and pencil

lamp

What to Do

Step ❶

Move the ball so that the pencil tip tilts away from the lamp. Where on the ball does the light shine most brightly?

Step ❷

Move the ball to the other side of the lamp. Do not change the pencil's direction or tilt. Where does the light shine most brightly?

Step ❸

Communicate what you observe.

Draw Conclusions

What season would it be for the side of the ball not facing the light?

Independent Inquiry

When you **communicate** your ideas, you tell or show others what you know. Communicate how light shines on a ball.

VOCABULARY
season

Focus Skill **CAUSE AND EFFECT**
Look for the cause of the seasons.

Earth's Orbit Around the Sun

It takes about 365 days for Earth to complete one orbit around the sun. Those 365 days make up Earth's year.

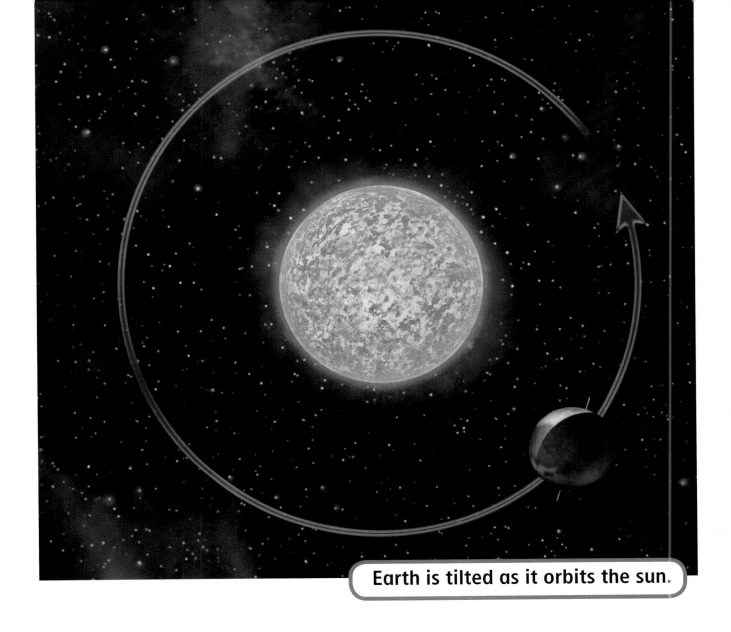

Earth is tilted as it orbits the sun.

Earth is always tilted in the same direction. But the part that is tilted toward the sun changes as Earth orbits the sun. At one time of the year, the north part of Earth is tilted toward the sun. At other times of the year, it is tilted away from the sun.

Focus Skill CAUSE AND EFFECT

Why is one part of Earth sometimes tilted toward the sun and sometimes tilted away from the sun?

337

Seasons Change

The part of Earth that is tilted toward the sun changes as Earth orbits the sun. This causes the seasons to change.

spring

summer

A **season** is a time of the year that has a certain kind of weather. Spring, summer, fall, and winter are seasons. They repeat in the same pattern each year.

 **CAUSE AND EFFECT**

What causes the seasons to change?

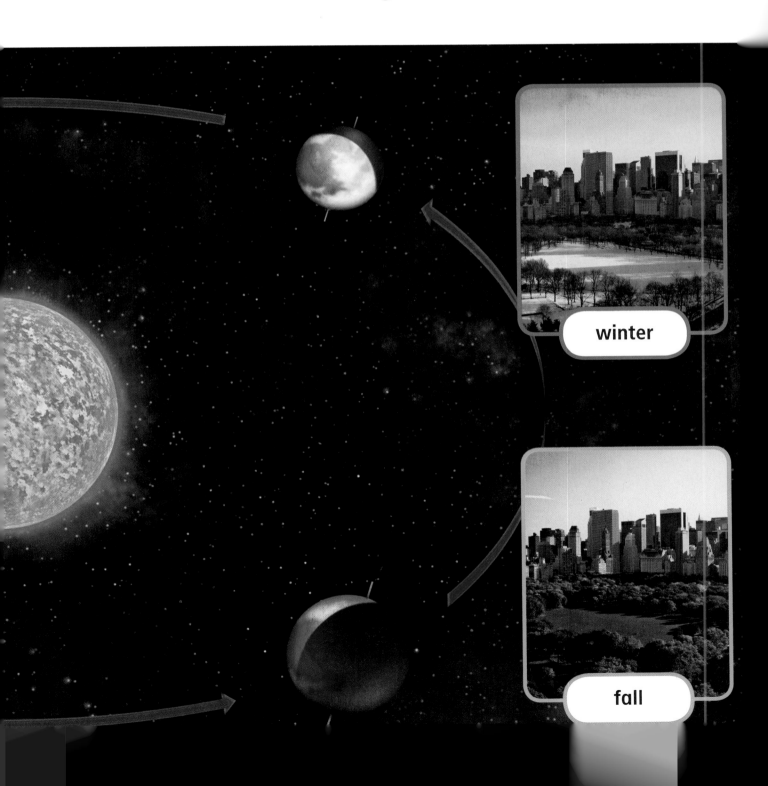

winter

fall

Why Seasons Change

When the part of Earth where you live is tilted toward the sun, it is summer. Sunlight hits that part of Earth directly. This causes warmer temperatures. There are more hours of daylight.

When the part of Earth where you live is tilted away from the sun, it is winter. Sunlight hits that part of Earth at a slant. This causes cooler temperatures. There are fewer hours of daylight.

Insta-Lab

Slanting Light

Shine a flashlight directly onto a sheet of paper. Now tilt the paper so that the light hits it at a slant. Tell what looks different about the light on the page.

(Focus Skill) CAUSE AND EFFECT

What happens when a part of Earth is tilted toward the sun?

Which day has the most hours of daylight? Why?

Hours of Daylight in Georgia

day

day	number of hours of daylight
March 21	12
June 21	14
September 21	12
December 21	9

0 1 2 3 4 5 6 7 8 9 10 11 12 13 14 15

number of hours of daylight

Essential Question

What causes the seasons?

In this lesson, you learned about Earth's orbit and why seasons change.

1.  **CAUSE AND EFFECT**
Make a chart like this one. Show the effects of the tilt of part of Earth toward the sun and away from the sun.

cause ⟶ effect

2. VOCABULARY How do the **seasons** form a pattern?

3. DRAW CONCLUSIONS As summer changes to fall, will there be more hours or fewer hours of daylight? How do you know?

4. SUMMARIZE Write two sentences that tell what this lesson is mostly about. Start with **When Earth is tilted.**

Test Prep

5. Why do the seasons change?

Make Connections

 Writing

Sentences About Seasons
Write about Earth's tilt at the beginning of each season where you live. Draw pictures to show the tilt in each season.

Seasons

Ellen Ochoa

In 1991, Ellen Ochoa became the first Latina astronaut. Since then, she has been in space four times. She has spent almost 1,000 hours in space.

The longest trip for Ellen Ochoa was an 11-day trip to space in 1999. She and her crew delivered supplies for the first astronauts who were going to live in the International Space Station.

► **ELLEN OCHOA**
► Astronaut

 Think and Write

How do you think Ellen Ochoa felt on her first trip into space?

▶ **DR. GEORGE ROBERT CARRUTHERS**

▶ Space scientist and inventor

George Robert Carruthers

What do things look like in space? Dr. George Robert Carruthers has helped people find out. He invented special cameras that are used on space missions. They help scientists learn more about space. Scientists use them to study the air around Earth to find out about things that are polluting it. They learned that oxygen on Earth is not all made by plants, as scientists once thought. Scientists also got new ideas about how stars form.

 Think and Write

As a young boy, Dr. Carruthers visited planetariums to see shows about space. He also belonged to a rocket club. What do these facts tell you about Dr. Carruthers?

343

Vocabulary Review

Use the terms below to complete the sentences. The page numbers tell you where to look if you need help.

solar system p. 312   **star** p. 314

planet p. 312   **constellation** p. 314

orbit p. 313   **rotates** p. 320

1. A path around something is an _____.

2. A huge ball of hot gases is a _____.

3. When something spins around, it _____.

4. The sun, all its planets, and the planets' moons mainly make up the _____.

5. A large ball of rock or gas that moves around the sun is a _____.

6. A group of stars that forms a pattern is a _____.

Check Understanding

7. When are the stars and planets in the sky?

    A only in the morning

    B only at night

    C only in the afternoon

    D all the time

8. Which detail about Earth's rotation is correct?

    F It causes the sun to move.

    G It causes winter to become spring.

    H It causes Earth to have day and night.

    J It causes summer to become fall.

Critical Thinking

9. What would happen if Earth were not tilted as it orbits?

10. Why do all parts of Earth not have light at the same time?

Tell how each picture shows the **Big Idea** for its chapter.

CHAPTER 7

Big Idea

Weather can be observed, measured, predicted, and compared.

CHAPTER 8

Big Idea

Earth is a planet. Changes happen on Earth and in the sky from day to night and from season to season.

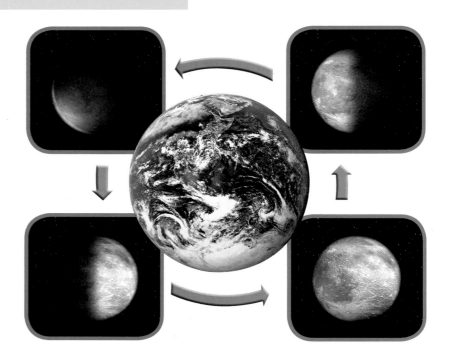

PHYSICAL SCIENCE

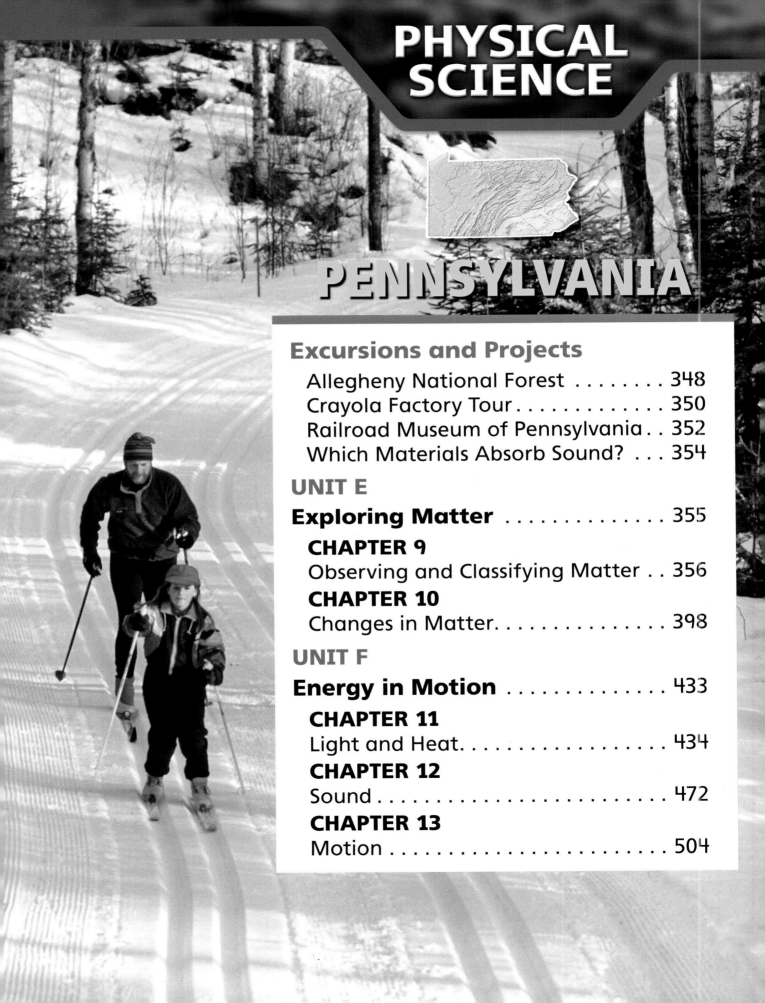

PENNSYLVANIA

Allegheny
National Forest

ALLEGHENY
NATIONAL FOREST REGION

Energy works in many ways in this forest. First, the sun's energy makes the ground warm. Next, the green leaves turn the sun's energy into food. Then, the deer eat the leaves and get the energy from the food. This energy helps them run and jump.

In the Forest

The Allegheny National Forest is in northwestern Pennsylvania. It is the only national forest in the state. The forest covers half a million acres and has lakes, mountains, and more than 700 miles of streams. In the water, you can see many kinds of fish. There are trout, bass, sunfish, and catfish. In the trees, there are many kinds of birds. Hawks and owls live here. There are also many songbirds. Roaming the woods are hares, foxes, minks, and bears.

Enjoying the Forest

People go to the forest to do many things. They hike on trails that go by lakes. They camp in the hills.

People use the park in the winter, too. They use snowshoes and skis. People ski the same trails they hike in the summer.

Think And Write

1 **Scientific Thinking** How does the park show ways energy is used?

2 **Scientific Thinking** What are some ways people use energy in the park?

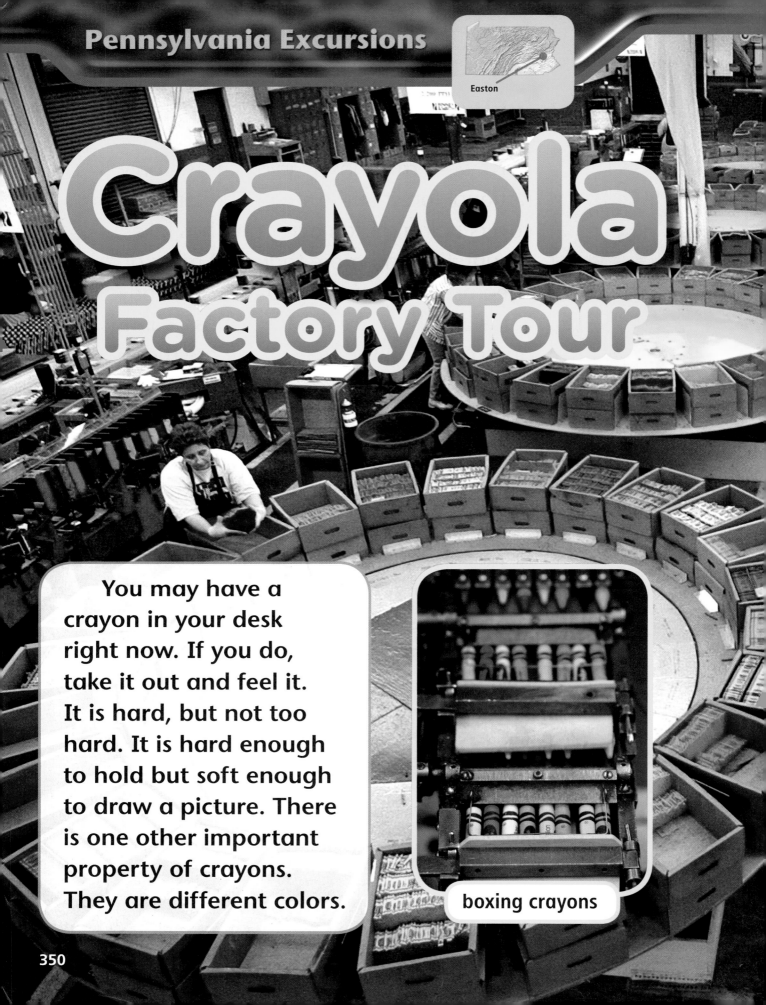

Easton

Crayola
Factory Tour

You may have a crayon in your desk right now. If you do, take it out and feel it. It is hard, but not too hard. It is hard enough to hold but soft enough to draw a picture. There is one other important property of crayons. They are different colors.

boxing crayons

350

See How Crayons Are Made

How are crayons made? This is the place to find out! Crayons are made of wax. The wax is melted. Then the color is put in the wax. The wax is put into crayon-shaped molds to cool. Paper labels are added, and the crayons are put into boxes. Then they are shipped to stores all over the world to be sold.

Other Things to Do

You can mix colors to make new ones. You can make your artwork into a book and take it home. Remember not to leave your crayons in the sun or they will melt!

Think And Write

❶ **Scientific Thinking** Why do you think the label is put on the crayon last?

❷ **Scientific Thinking** How would you tell someone what a crayon is like?

melted wax

Strasburg

RAILROAD MUSEUM
OF PENNSYLVANIA

475

Trains have been a big part of Pennsylvania for many, many years. They haul coal from the mines. They take food to and from our state. They also take people where they want to go. In this museum, you can find out how railroads got started in our state. You can find out how they were built and how they grew. You can find out more about how trains are used today.

What to See at the Museum

This museum started as a way to show how important trains are to Pennsylvania. Inside, you can see more than 100 trains. You can look at the engines that power the trains. Older trains ran by burning coal. Trains today burn diesel, a kind of oil. You can see the kinds of cars engines pulled long ago and today.

steam engine

What to Do at the Museum

You can go inside some of the cars at the museum and see where people sat and slept long ago. You can see inside the cab of an engine.

Across from the museum, you can ride on an old steam train. Some of the cars have seats and windows for people. Other cars are open for carrying goods. You can get a feeling for what it was like to ride on a train long ago.

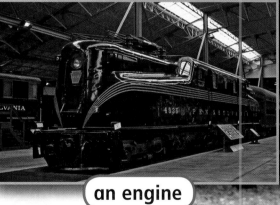

an engine

Think And Write

1. **Scientific Thinking** How have trains helped people meet their needs?

2. **Scientific Thinking** How have trains changed?

Project — Which Materials Absorb Sound?

Materials

- battery radio
- cardboard box with lid
- towel
- different kinds of cloth
- newspaper
- plastic bags
- sweater
- pillow

Procedure

1. Turn on the radio. Play music loudly. Put the radio inside the box and close it. Is the music as loud as it was?

2. Take the radio from the box. Cover it with different kinds of material. Which one works best at making the sound not as loud?

3. Turn the radio to a talk program. Try the same test. Does the same material work as well as before?

Draw Conclusions

1. Why do some materials work better than others at making the sound not as loud?

2. How might a person who is building a music hall use what you found out?

Exploring Matter

Unit Inquiry

Solids in Water

As you do this unit, you will learn about matter.
Plan and do a test. Find out how water temperature
changes the way solids dissolve.

Observing and Classifying Matter

What's the Big Idea?

There are three states of matter: solid, liquid, and gas.

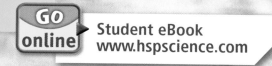
GO online Student eBook
www.hspscience.com

What do yOU wonder?

What kinds of matter are the sand, the sea, and the air? Think about the **Big Idea** to help you answer.

357

What Is Matter?

Investigate to find out about different kinds of matter.

Read and Learn about matter.

Fast Fact

Matter Everywhere

Everything in the world is made up of matter. Ice is solid matter. It has a shape. Some artists carve ice into interesting shapes. One way to compare objects is to observe their shapes.

Matter is the material all things are made of. Matter can be a solid, a liquid, or a gas. (p. 362)

A **property** is one part of what something is like. Color, size, and shape are each a property. (p. 364)

Mass is the amount of matter in an object. Mass can be measured by using a tool called a balance. (p. 364)

Kinds of Matter

Guided Inquiry

Ask a Question

What matter do you see in this picture?
Investigate to find out. Then read and learn to find out more.

Get Ready

Inquiry Skill Tip

When you compare things, you see how they are alike and how they are different.

You need

jar of water with lid on

zip-top bag filled with air

block

What to Do

Step ① ━━━━━━━━━━━━━

Gently shake the jar of water. Observe any changes to the water.

Step ② ━━━━━━━━━━━━━

Gently press the bag filled with air. Observe any changes to the air.

Step ③

Turn the block on its side. Squeeze it. Observe any changes to the block.
Compare the changes to the water, the air, and the block.

Draw Conclusions

How were the changes to the air and the water alike?

Independent Inquiry

Comparing things helps you see how they are alike and different. Compare the color and shape of water, air, and a block.

VOCABULARY
matter
property
mass

COMPARE AND CONTRAST
Look for ways different forms of matter
are alike and ways they are different.

Forms of Matter

All things are made of **matter**. The
books you read, the air you breathe,
and the water you drink are all made of
matter. Even people are made of matter.

What things in this picture are made
of matter?

Matter has three forms. It can be a solid, a liquid, or a gas. The balloons, cars, hills, trees, and grass are solids. The water in the lake is a liquid. The air in the sky and inside the balloons is a gas.

Focus Skill **COMPARE AND CONTRAST**

How are the objects in this picture alike? How are they different?

Properties of Matter

Matter has properties. A **property** is one part of what something is like. It describes the matter that the thing is made of.

All matter has two main properties—it takes up space, and it has mass. **Mass** is the amount of matter in an object.

Matter has other properties. Color, size, and shape are properties of matter. The way something feels is also a property.

Find the object in the picture that is hard and bumpy and is shaped like a star. Now find the object that is shiny and smooth and is red, blue, and yellow. Properties can help you tell one object from another.

 COMPARE AND CONTRAST
What two main properties do all kinds of matter have?

Matter and Space

Choose three classroom objects. Arrange them in order from the one that takes up the least space to the one that takes up the most space. Tell a classmate why you ordered the objects the way you did.

Measuring Mass

You can use a balance to find the mass of a solid. Put a solid object on one side of the balance. Add masses to the other side until both sides are even. Each mass has a number on it. Add the numbers to find the mass of the object you chose.

(Focus Skill) **COMPARE AND CONTRAST**

Do the masses have more or less mass than this shell?

What is matter?

In this lesson, you learned about forms of matter, properties of matter, and how to measure mass.

1.  **COMPARE AND CONTRAST** Make a chart like this one. Tell how the three forms of matter are alike and how they are different.

| alike |—| different |

2. VOCABULARY Describe the block by naming some of its **properties**.

3. DRAW CONCLUSIONS What can you use to tell objects apart?

4. SUMMARIZE Use your chart to write a lesson summary.

Test Prep

5. How can you measure the mass of a solid?

Make Connections

 Writing

List of Clues
Draw a picture of a classroom object. On the other side of the paper, write a list of its properties as clues. Ask a classmate to read your clues and guess the object.

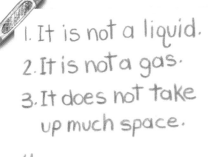

1. It is not a liquid.
2. It is not a gas.
3. It does not take up much space.
4.

What Are Solids?

Investigate to find out how to measure a solid.

Read and Learn about what solids are.

Fast Fact

Measuring Matter

Sculptures are made from solid matter, such as wood, clay, metal, and stone. Measuring solid objects can help you find out their size and mass.

A **solid** is the only form of matter that has its own shape. (p. 372)

Texture is the way something feels when you touch it. (p. 373)

A **centimeter** is a unit used to measure how long a solid is. Centimeters are marked on many rulers. (p. 375)

Measure a Solid

Ask a Question

How can you find out which toy truck has more mass? Investigate to find out. Then read and learn to find out more.

Get Ready

Inquiry Skill Tip

You can use a balance to measure the mass of a solid.

You need

4 objects

balance

What to Do

Step ①

Use the balance to **measure** the mass of each object.

Step ②

Put the objects in order from the least mass to the most mass.

Step ③

Make a chart to show the order of the objects from least mass to most mass.

Draw Conclusions

Did the size of the object affect its mass?

Independent Inquiry

You can use a balance to **measure** the mass of a solid. Measure the mass of a box of crayons and four other classroom objects.

VOCABULARY
solid
texture
centimeter

 **COMPARE AND CONTRAST**
Look for ways solids are alike and ways
they are different.

Properties of Solids

A solid is a form of matter. All matter
has mass and takes up space. A **solid** is the
only form of matter that has its own shape.
The shape of a solid will not change unless
you cut it, bend it, break it, or change it in
another way.

You can see and feel a solid. Some solids are hard, and some are soft. Solids can have different colors, sizes, and shapes. They can have different textures, too. **Texture** is the way something feels when you touch it.

COMPARE AND CONTRAST

How are solids alike? How are they different?

Insta-Lab

Sort Classroom Objects

With a partner, gather some classroom objects. Take turns describing their properties. Then sort the objects in different ways, such as by color, by shape, by size, and by texture.

Measuring Solids

Solids do not all have the same mass. You can use a balance to measure the mass of a solid. This boy is measuring the mass of a clay cat.

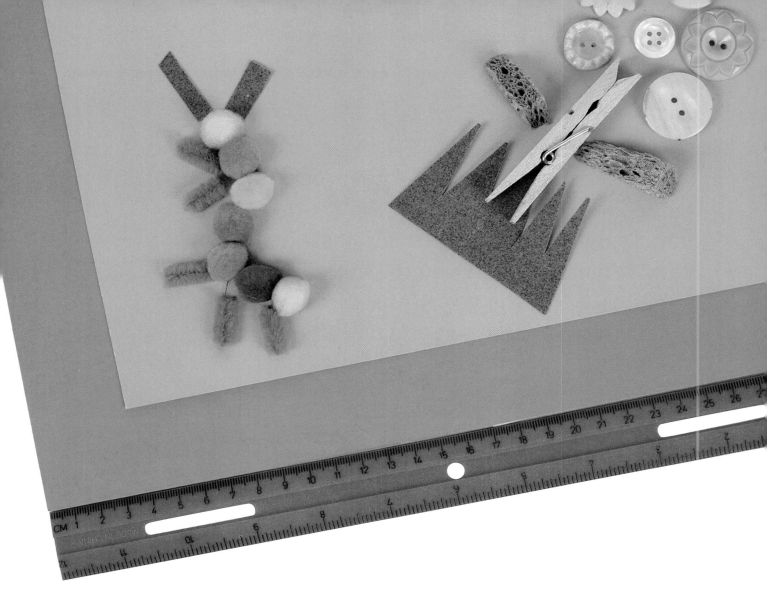

You can measure how long, high, and wide a solid is. You can use a ruler, a meterstick, or a yardstick to measure.

A **centimeter** is a unit used to measure length. An inch is also a unit of length. This ruler measures both centimeters and inches.

Focus Skill COMPARE AND CONTRAST

How are a balance and a ruler alike?
How are they different?

375

Different Textures

Some rocks feel smooth. Other rocks feel rough. You can compare the textures of rocks by looking at them and feeling them. A hand lens lets you see more details. How are the textures of these rocks different? How can you tell?

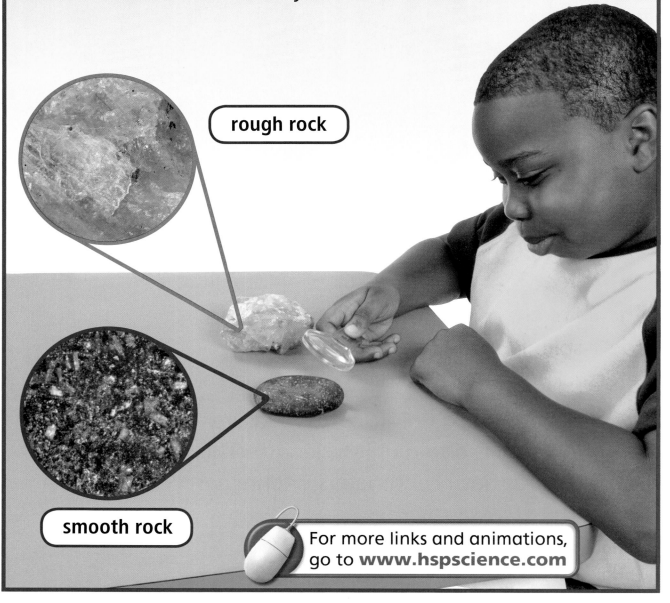

rough rock

smooth rock

For more links and animations, go to **www.hspscience.com**

Essential Question

What are solids?

In this lesson, you learned about properties of solids, about different textures, and how to measure solids.

1. (Focus Skill) **COMPARE AND CONTRAST** Make a chart like this one. Tell how solids are alike and how they can be different.

> alike ——— different

2. VOCABULARY Use the term **centimeter** to tell about this picture.

3. DRAW CONCLUSIONS How are a rock, a block, and a ball alike?

4. SUMMARIZE Use the chart to tell what this lesson is mostly about. Tell about two ways to describe matter.

Test Prep

5. What property does a solid have that other forms of matter do **NOT** have?

   A It has mass.
   B It takes up space.
   C It has its own shape.
   D It can be measured.

Make Connections

123 Math

Measure How Big Around
Wrap a string around the outside of an object. Measure the length of the string with a ruler to find how big around the object is. Then draw a picture of the object, and record how big around it is.

The ball is 26 centimeters around.

Investigate to find out how to measure a liquid.

Read and Learn about liquids.

Essential Question

What Are Liquids?

Fast Fact

Changing Matter

Iguazú Falls, in South America, is one of the largest waterfalls in the world. The shape of the falling water is always changing. Making inferences helps you figure out why matter changes.

A **liquid** is a form of matter that takes the shape of its container. (p. 382)

Volume is the amount of space something takes up. (p. 384)

A **milliliter** is a unit used to measure the volume of a liquid. Milliliters are marked on many measuring cups. (p. 384)

Measure a Liquid

Guided Inquiry

Ask a Question

Is there enough orange juice to fill the two glasses? Investigate to find out. Then read and learn to find out more.

Get Ready

Inquiry Skill Tip

When you infer, you use what you have observed to figure out what happened.

You need

colored water

measuring cup

3 different clear containers

black marker

What to Do

Step 1

Measure $\frac{1}{2}$ cup water. Pour the water into a container. Mark the level on the outside of the container.

Step 2

Repeat Step 1 for the other two containers.

Step 3

Observe the water level. Is it the same in all three containers? Why or why not? What can you **infer**?

Draw Conclusions

What if you poured 1 cup into each container. Would it be the same in all three?

Independent Inquiry

When you **infer**, you use what you have observed to figure out what happened. Infer about the amount of water in different containers.

MAIN IDEA AND DETAILS
Look for details about the properties of liquids.

Properties of Liquids

Liquids are a form of matter. Like all matter, a **liquid** has mass and takes up space. A liquid does not have its own shape. It takes the shape of its container.

A liquid in a bottle has the same shape as the bottle. If you tilt the bottle, the liquid changes shape. If you pour the liquid into a glass, it takes the shape of the glass.

You can see and feel a liquid. If you pour liquid from one container into another, its shape changes. The amount of liquid stays the same. The amount does not change unless you add more liquid or take some away.

 **MAIN IDEA AND DETAILS**

What shape does a liquid always take?

Measuring Liquids

You can measure the volume of a liquid. **Volume** is the amount of space a liquid takes up. A **milliliter** is a unit used to measure the volume of a liquid. An ounce is a unit of volume, too.

A measuring cup may show milliliters on one side and ounces on the other side.

 **MAIN IDEA AND DETAILS**

What can you use to measure the volume of a liquid?

Measure Two Ways

Use a measuring cup to find out about how many milliliters equal 5 ounces. Tell a classmate how you found the amount.

Essential Question

What are liquids?

In this lesson, you learned about properties of liquids and how to measure liquids.

1. (Focus Skill) **MAIN IDEA AND DETAILS**
Make a chart like this one. Fill in details about this main idea. **Liquids are a form of matter.**

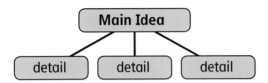

2. VOCABULARY Use the terms **volume, liquid,** and **milliliter** to tell about this picture.

3. DRAW CONCLUSIONS If you pour a glass of water into a bowl, would it still be the same amount of water?

4. SUMMARIZE Write two sentences that tell what this lesson is about.

Test Prep

5. How do you know that a liquid does not have its own shape?

Make Connections

 Health

Measure Your Liquids

Liquids help the body stay healthy. You should drink six to eight cups of water or other liquids each day Keep a chart for a few days. Record each time you drink a liquid and about how much you drink. Share your chart.

7:00   1 cup
12:00 2 cups
3:00   1 cup
6:30   2 cups
8:00   1 cup

Investigate to find out how to measure a gas.

Read and Learn about gases.

Essential Question

What Are Gases?

Fast Fact

Shaping Air
You can twist balloons into different shapes because the air inside does not have its own shape. Making inferences can help you learn about air.

Gas is the only form of matter that always fills all the space of its container. (p. 390)

Measure a Gas

Ask a Question

Can you measure the mass of a balloon?

Investigate to find out. Then read and learn to find out more.

Get Ready

Inquiry Skill Tip

When you infer, you use what you observed to figure out why something happened.

You need

balance

balloon filled with air

balloon without air

What to Do

Step ①

Place the balloon filled with air on one side of the balance. Place the balloon without air on the other side.

Step ②

Observe both balloons. What can you **infer** about why their masses are different? Record what you **infer**.

Step ③

Communicate to a classmate what you **infer**.

Draw Conclusions

Would your answer be different if both balloons were full of air?

Independent Inquiry

When you **infer**, you use what you observed to figure out why something happened. What would you infer about the mass of three balloons?

VOCABULARY
gas

Look for details about the properties of gases.

Gases and Air

Gases are a form of matter. Like all matter, a **gas** takes up space and has mass. It is the only kind of matter that always fills all the space of its container. When you blow up a balloon, the gas spreads out inside. It takes the shape of the balloon. A gas does not have its own shape.

Gases are in this drink. Can you find them?

Air is made up of gases. It is all around you. Often you cannot see, smell, or feel the air around you. But you can see and feel what it does. Moving air lifts the girl's hair. Moving air also makes a pinwheel spin.

MAIN IDEA AND DETAILS

What happens when air is put into a balloon?

Insta-Lab

Observe Air

Tightly pack a paper towel into the bottom of a cup. Turn the cup upside down. Push it straight down into a bowl of water. Then pull it straight out. What happens to the paper towel? Why?

Comparing Forms of Matter

The chart below tells about the three forms of matter. How are they alike? How are they different?

 **MAIN IDEA AND DETAILS**

What are two details about each type of matter?

Forms of Matter			
	solid	liquid	gas
mass	has mass	has mass	has mass
space	takes up space	takes up space	takes up space
shape	has its own shape	takes the shape of its container	spreads out to fill its container
ways it can be measured	mass—balance size—ruler	mass—balance volume—measuring cup	mass—balance

Essential Question

What are gases?

In this lesson, you learned about air and other gases.

1. **MAIN IDEA AND DETAILS**
Make a chart like this one.
Fill in details about this main
idea. **Gases are a form of
matter.**

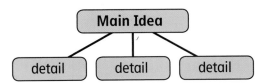

2. **VOCABULARY** Use the term
gas to tell about a balloon.

3. **DRAW CONCLUSIONS** What
shape is the air inside a
bubble?

4. **SUMMARIZE** Use your chart to
tell what this lesson is mostly
about. Start with **Gas is
matter because.**

Test Prep

5. How is a gas like all matter?
   A It takes up space.
   B It has its own shape.
   C You can always see it.
   D You can always feel it.

Make Connections

 Art

Make a Windsock
Decorate a sheet of paper. Tape it together
to make a tube. Tape paper strips to one
end. Make three holes in the other end. Tie
string in the holes. Then tie the windsock
to a stick. Show how wind makes the
windsock move.

Albert Einstein

► **ALBERT EINSTEIN**
► Scientist

Albert Einstein is one of the most famous scientists in history. It might surprise you to learn that he didn't do well in some subjects in school. He loved math and science, though.

As he grew up, Albert Einstein read a lot because he wanted to learn about the things around him. He thought about the things he could see. He also thought about things that were much too small to see. He used his imagination to look at things in new ways. He thought about matter in ways that no one ever had before.

 Think and Write

How can using your imagination help you learn new things?

394

▶ **DR. AYANNA HOWARD**

▶ Robotics engineer at the Jet Propulsion Lab, California Institute of Technology

▶ Works on software for robots

Ayanna Howard

Dr. Ayanna Howard works on making robots. Someday her robot SmartNav may walk on Mars! Dr. Howard wants her robot to be able to think like a human.

SmartNav can already do some things people can do. It can tell sand from stone or concrete. Doing this will help SmartNav move on Mars.

Dr. Howard also helps girls with math and science. She hopes that girls will share her interest in working with robots.

 Think and Write

How might the work of earlier space scientists help Ayanna Howard?

Vocabulary Review

Use the terms below to complete the sentences. The page numbers tell you where to look if you need help.

matter p. 362   texture p. 373

mass p. 364   liquid p. 382

solid p. 372   gas p. 390

1. Matter that has its own shape is a _____ .

2. The way something feels is its _____ .

3. Everything in the world is made up of _____ .

4. Matter that always fills all the space of its container is a _____ .

5. A balance measures an object's _____ .

6. Matter you can see that does not have its own shape is a _____ .

Check Understanding

7. How are all the things in the picture the same?

A They are all liquids.

B They are all solids.

C They are all gases.

D They are all made of matter.

8. What are two properties of all matter?

F Matter has mass and color.

G Matter has color and its own shape.

H Matter has mass and takes up space.

J Matter has texture and no shape of its own.

Critical Thinking

9. Jon has a fish tank. Tell how it has all three kinds of matter in it.

The **Big Idea**

10. How can you use a ruler, a balance, and a measuring cup to learn about matter?

What's
the
Big
Idea?

Matter can change in
two ways.

Essential Questions

Lesson 1

How Can Matter Change?

Lesson 2

How Can Water Change?

Lesson 3

What Are Other Changes to Matter?

GO
online

Student eBook
www.hspscience.com

What do yOU wonder?

Water sometimes changes to ice. How does this connect to the **Big Idea**?

Investigate to find out how to make a mixture.

Read and Learn about how matter can change.

Essential Question

How Can Matter Change?

Fast Fact

Many Mixtures

The children's pasta with sauce and cheese is a mixture. The green salad is also a mixture. You can communicate about foods you like when you make tasty mixtures.

A **mixture** is a mix of different kinds of matter. Substances in a mixture do not become other substances. (p. 404)

401

Make a Mixture

Guided Inquiry

Ask a Question

This salad is a mixture. How can you make a mixture? Investigate to find out. Then read and learn to find out more.

Get Ready

You need

dried fruits and seeds

measuring cup

zip-top bag

What to Do

Step

Use the measuring cup to measure the same amounts of dried fruits and seeds.

Step ②

Put the foods into the bag. Close the bag tightly, and shake it.

Step ③

Observe. What has changed? **Communicate** to your classmates what you see.

Draw Conclusions

What has stayed the same in the mixture?

Independent Inquiry

When you **communicate** your observations, you share with others what you have learned. Communicate your observations as you separate the mixture you made for the Investigate activity.

VOCABULARY
mixture

 **CAUSE AND EFFECT**
Look for ways matter can change. Find the cause of each change.

Mixing Matter

When you mix two or more kinds of matter, you make a **mixture**. Solids, liquids, and gases can all be parts of mixtures. Fruit salad is a mixture of solids. You make it by mixing pieces of fruit. You can separate fruit salad into pieces. Each piece is the same size and shape as it was in the mixture. Substances you put in a mixture do not become new substances.

Lemonade is a mixture. You make it with water, lemon juice, and sugar. The sugar is a solid. You mix it with the two liquids. You no longer see the sugar, but it is there. If you take a sip, you will taste the sugar.

 **CAUSE AND EFFECT**

What happens to fruit pieces when you mix them together?

Mix It Up

Mix four spoonfuls of cornstarch with two spoonfuls of water. Roll the mixture in your hands. Pour it from hand to hand. What happens? Describe the cornstarch and water before and after you mixed them.

Kinds of Changes

You change matter when you cut it. Cutting a watermelon changes its size and shape. Look at these other ways to change matter.

Focus Skill CAUSE AND EFFECT

How does matter change when you cut it or break it?

Break it.

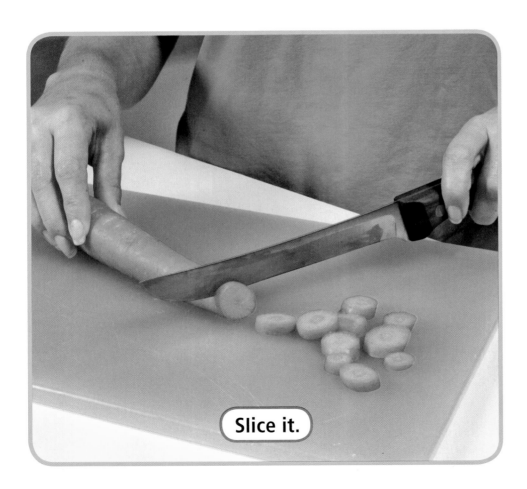

Slice it.

Shape it.

Tear it.

Cut it.

Measuring Matter

When you change only the shape of matter, its mass stays the same. The pieces of cheese on both sides of this balance were once alike. They were blocks that had the same shape and mass. Then one block of cheese was changed. It was cut into cubes. Its shape changed. But the balance shows that its mass did not change.

(Focus Skill) **CAUSE AND EFFECT**

What stayed the same when the cheese was cut into cubes? How do you know it stayed the same?

Essential Question

How can matter change?

In this lesson, you learned about changes to matter.

1.  **CAUSE AND EFFECT** Make a chart like this one. Show the effects of tearing, cutting, slicing, and breaking food.

cause ⟶ effect

2. VOCABULARY Use the term **mixture** to tell about the picture.

3. DRAW CONCLUSIONS How could you find out if the mass of an apple was the same as or different from the mass of an orange?

4. SUMMARIZE Write two sentences that tell what this lesson is about.

Test Prep

5. When the shape of matter is changed, what stays the same?

Make Connections

 Writing

Snack Recipe
Make up a healthful snack that is a mixture of different foods. Write your recipe. List what you need. Write steps to tell how to make it. Share your recipe with your classmates.

Margie's Munchy Mix

What you need

1 cup pumpkin seeds
1 cup raisins
cereal

How Can Water Change?

Investigate to find out what freezing does to water.

Read and Learn about how water can change.

Fast Fact

Changing Water

Water is the only matter that is naturally found in three forms on Earth. The forms are solid, liquid, and gas. You can predict which form the ice in this pond will become when it gets warmer.

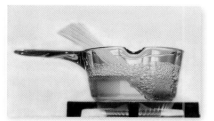

Evaporation is the change of water from a liquid to a gas. Evaporation happens when heat is added to liquid water. (p. 417)

Water vapor is water in the form of a gas. (p. 417)

Condensation is the change of water from a gas to a liquid. Condensation happens when heat is taken away from water vapor. (p. 418)

411

What Freezing Does

Guided Inquiry

Ask a Question

When the sun comes out, what will happen to this snowman? Investigate to find out. Then read and learn to find out more.

Get Ready

Inquiry Skill Tip
When you predict, you tell what you think will happen.

You need

plastic tub with lid

water

marker

What to Do

Step 1

Fill a plastic tub halfway with water. Mark the water level on the side of the tub.

Step 2

Put a lid on the tub. Place the tub in the freezer. **Predict** what will happen to the water.

Step 3

Wait one day. Remove the tub from the freezer and observe.

Draw Conclusions

Did the water change? Did the tub change? How did they change?

Independent Inquiry

When you **predict**, you tell what you think will happen. Predict what will happen to the tub of frozen water if you set it in a sunny place for a few days.

VOCABULARY
evaporation
water vapor
condensation

(Focus Skill) **CAUSE AND EFFECT**

Look for the causes that change water into a solid, a liquid, and a gas.

Freezing

Water has three forms. It can be a solid, a liquid, or a gas.

Water changes from a liquid to a solid when enough heat is taken away from it. The water freezes and becomes ice. Ice is water in its solid form.

The tray is filled with juice. Juice is mostly water. How will it change when it freezes?

The juice is no longer a liquid. It has changed to a solid. It is now an ice pop. Matter that is a solid has its own shape.

Focus Skill CAUSE AND EFFECT

What caused the juice to change from a liquid to a solid?

Melting

The ice pop is now melting. Warm air is adding heat to the ice. Ice melts when its temperature is high enough.

The juice changes from a solid to a liquid. It no longer has its own shape.

 **CAUSE AND EFFECT**

Why is the ice pop melting?

Which Melts Faster?

Set out two plates. Put one ice cube on each plate. Place a lamp above one of the plates. Wait five minutes. Which ice cube melted faster? Why?

Evaporation and Boiling

Water changes from a liquid to a gas when enough heat is added to it. This change is called **evaporation**. Water that is a gas is called **water vapor**. You cannot see water vapor. It is in the air.

Water boils when its temperature gets high enough. The boiling water in this pot is evaporating. As long as the water keeps boiling, it will continue to evaporate.

 **CAUSE AND EFFECT**
What causes water to change to a gas?

Condensation

Water vapor changes from a gas to a liquid when heat is taken away from it. This change is called **condensation**.

This glass is filled with a cold drink. It takes heat away from the air around it. This changes the water vapor in the air into a liquid. The tiny drops of water on the outside of the glass show that water has condensed from water vapor.

Focus Skill CAUSE AND EFFECT

What caused water drops to form on the outside of the glass?

Essential Question

How can water change?

In this lesson, you learned about freezing, melting, evaporation, boiling, and condensation of water.

1.  **CAUSE AND EFFECT**
Make a chart like this one. Tell how water changes.

$$\boxed{\text{cause}} \longrightarrow \boxed{\text{effect}}$$

2. VOCABULARY Use the terms **water vapor** and **condensation** to tell about this picture.

3. DRAW CONCLUSIONS Can ice that becomes a liquid change back to a solid? Explain.

4. SUMMARIZE Use the chart to tell what this lesson is mostly about.

Test Prep

5. How can you change water to a gas?

   A Take heat away.

   B Condense it.

   C Add heat.

   D Make ice.

Make Connections

 Math

Measure and Compare
Measure the temperature of a glass of water. Then measure the temperature of a bowl of ice Compare. Does the water or the ice have the lower temperature?

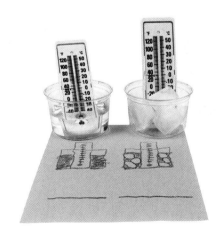

Essential Question

What Are Other Changes to Matter?

Investigate to find out one way matter can change.

Read and Learn about other ways matter can change.

Fast Fact

Changing Matter

You can tell how hot parts of a fire are by looking at their colors. The blue part is the hottest. Fire is so hot that it can change one kind of matter into another. Drawing conclusions can help you figure out why matter changes.

Burning is the change of a substance into ashes and smoke. (p. 424)

How Matter Can Change

Ask a Question

How does this egg change as it is cooked?

Investigate to find out. Then read and learn to find out more.

Get Ready

Inquiry Skill Tip

Use your observations and what you know to draw conclusions.

You need

black plastic bowl

foil

gelatin cube

What to Do

Step 1

Place the foil, shiny side up, in the bowl.

Step 2

Place the gelatin cube on the foil in the bowl. Place the bowl outside in a sunny spot.

Step 3

Wait one hour. Observe the gelatin cube. Can you **draw conclusions** from what you observed? Explain.

Draw Conclusions

If you put the gelatin cube in the refrigerator what would happen?

Independent Inquiry

Use your observations and what you know to **draw conclusions**. Draw conclusions about heat and food.

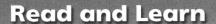

Focus Skill **CAUSE AND EFFECT**

Look for the causes and effects of burning and cooking.

Burning and Cooking

Fire and cooking change matter into different matter. The new matter can not change back into what it was before.

The fire is burning this wood. **Burning** the wood changes it into ashes and smoke. The ashes and smoke can not change back into wood.

Cooking heats food. The heat changes the marshmallows. They change from white to brown. They can not change back to white.

The meat and vegetables were raw, or uncooked. Cooking changed them. Their color, shape, texture, size, and taste are different. They can never be raw again.

(Focus Skill) CAUSE AND EFFECT

How and why does meat change when it is cooked?

Uncooked and Cooked

Draw pictures to show what spaghetti looks like before and after it is cooked. Tell a classmate how the spaghetti changes.

Making Muffins

1. Mix the ingredients.

2. Pour the mixture into a pan.

3. Bake the mixture.

What changes do you see? What caused these changes?

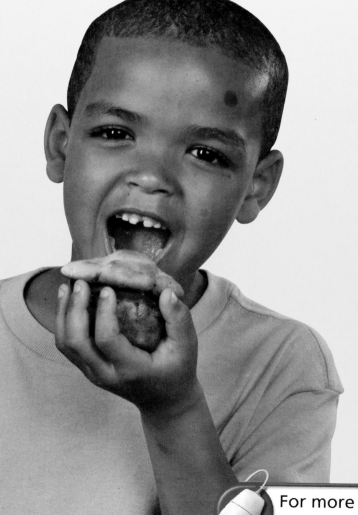

For more links and animations, go to **www.hspscience.com**

Essential Question

What are other changes to matter?

In this lesson, you learned about other changes to matter, such as burning and cooking.

1.  **CAUSE AND EFFECT**
Make a chart like this one. Show the effects of burning and cooking.

cause ⟶ effect

2. VOCABULARY Use the term **burning** to tell about this picture.

3. DRAW CONCLUSIONS
If you make scrambled eggs, what kind of change has taken place?

4. SUMMARIZE Use the chart to write a summary of this lesson.

Test Prep

5. What happens when paper burns?

A Its shape stays the same.
B Its size stays the same.
C Its matter changes.
D Its color stays the same.

Make Connections

 Art

Before and After
Draw pictures of a food before and after it is cooked. Tell about the food's texture, size, color, shape, and taste. Share your work with a classmate.

Dough

Bread

Up, Up, and Away

You may have heard of flying squirrels, or maybe even flying ants. But have you ever heard of a flying dog?

Meet Buster the terrier. Buster has visited about 30 states, mostly from hundreds of feet above the ground in a hot-air balloon.

Not Afraid of Heights

Buster's owner, Don Edwards, owns a hot-air balloon business in Florida. His dog loves to take to the air with him. Buster is a great flier, says his owner. Even the loud noise of the balloon's burner does not bother him.

Buster, who always wears a leash when in the balloon's gondola, or basket, can't wait to fly. His owner says, "When Buster flies, he is like a little kid."

How It Works

The burner is used to heat up the air inside the balloon's giant, colorful envelope. Hot air is less dense than cold air and makes the balloon rise. To keep the balloon from sinking, the air inside the balloon must be reheated from time to time. The pilot can reheat it by firing the burner.

 Think and Write

What makes a hot-air balloon float upward into the sky?

Find out more. Log on to www.hspscience.com

Vocabulary Review

Use the terms to complete the sentences. The page numbers tell you where to look if you need help.

mixture p. 404   **water vapor** p. 417

evaporation p. 417   **condensation** p. 418

1. When water changes from a liquid to a gas, the change is called _____.

2. Water in its gas form is called _____.

3. A mix of two or more things is a _____.

4. When water changes from a gas to a liquid, the change is called _____.

Check Understanding

5. How does water change when it is heated?

A It changes from a liquid to a solid.

B It changes from a gas to a solid.

C It changes from a liquid to a gas.

D It changes from a gas to a liquid.

6. What caused the loaf of bread to  change?

F burning

G cutting

H freezing

J mixing

Critical Thinking

7. What changes will these icicles go through to become water vapor?

The **Big Idea**

8. In what ways does an egg change when it is cooked?

Tell how each picture shows the **Big Idea** for its chapter.

CHAPTER
9

Big Idea

There are three states of matter: solid, liquid, and gas.

CHAPTER
10

Big Idea

Matter can change in two ways.

Energy in Motion

Unit Inquiry

Metals and Magnets

As you do this unit, you will learn about energy and motion. Plan and do a test. Find out how magnets make things move.

CHAPTER 11 Light and Heat

What's the Big Idea?

Light and heat are forms of energy.

Essential Questions

Lesson 1

What Is Energy?

Lesson 2

What Is Light?

Lesson 3

What Is Heat?

Student eBook
www.hspscience.com

Why do people make fires
in fireplaces? How does this
connect to the Big Idea?

Investigate to find out about energy from wind.

Read and Learn about what energy is.

Essential Question

What Is Energy?

Fast Fact

Wind Energy

A windmill's blades turn when wind pushes on them. This wind energy can be used to pump water out of the ground. You can communicate other ways people use wind for energy.

Energy is something that can cause matter to move or change. Heat, light, and sound are forms of energy. (p. 440)

Heat is energy that makes things warmer. Heat can be used to cook food and to melt things. (p. 440)

Light is a form of energy that lets you see. The sun and fires give off light energy. (p. 441)

Sound is energy you can hear. Sounds are made when objects vibrate. (p. 441)

Solar energy is energy from the sun. (p. 442)

Electricity is a form of energy. People produce electricity by using energy from other sources. (p. 444)

437

Energy from Wind

Ask a Question

What does this sailboat need in order to move?
Investigate to find out. Then read and learn to find out more.

Get Ready

Inquiry Skill Tip

You decide how you will experiment when you plan an investigation.

You need

toy car

clay

toothpicks

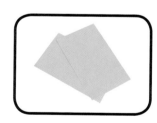

paper

What to Do

Step ① —

Plan an investigation.
Think of a way to use the clay, toothpicks, and paper to make a sail for the toy car.

Step ② —

Carry out the plan you made in Step 1.

Step ③

Blow on the sail. Observe what happens.

Draw Conclusions

What made the car move? Communicate your answer to a classmate.

Independent Inquiry

When you **plan an investigation** you decide how you will experiment. How else can you make the toy car move?

VOCABULARY
energy
heat
light
sound
solar energy
electricity

 **MAIN IDEA AND DETAILS**
Look for details about the forms of energy and about where energy comes from.

Energy

Energy is something that can cause matter to move or change. Energy has different forms. Heat, light, and sound are some forms of energy.

Heat is energy that makes things warmer. People use heat to warm their homes and cook their food. Heat can boil water and melt things, such as wax and ice. Heat can also burn things.

Heat makes water boil.

Pittsburgh, Pennsylvania

Light is energy that lets you see. The sun gives off light. Fires and electric lights give off light, too.

Sound is energy that you can hear. You hear sound when it travels to your ears. What kind of energy is the lion producing?

Focus Skill **MAIN IDEA AND DETAILS**
What are some forms of energy?

Where Energy Comes From

Almost all energy on Earth comes from the sun. Energy from the sun is called **solar energy**. Most living things need solar energy to live. They need the sun's heat to stay warm. Plants use the sun's light to make their food. People and animals eat the plants to get energy.

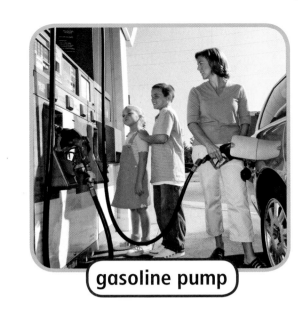

gasoline pump

Energy also comes from wind and moving water. They can make things move by pushing on them. How do wind and water move the kiteboard?

sun

kiteboarding

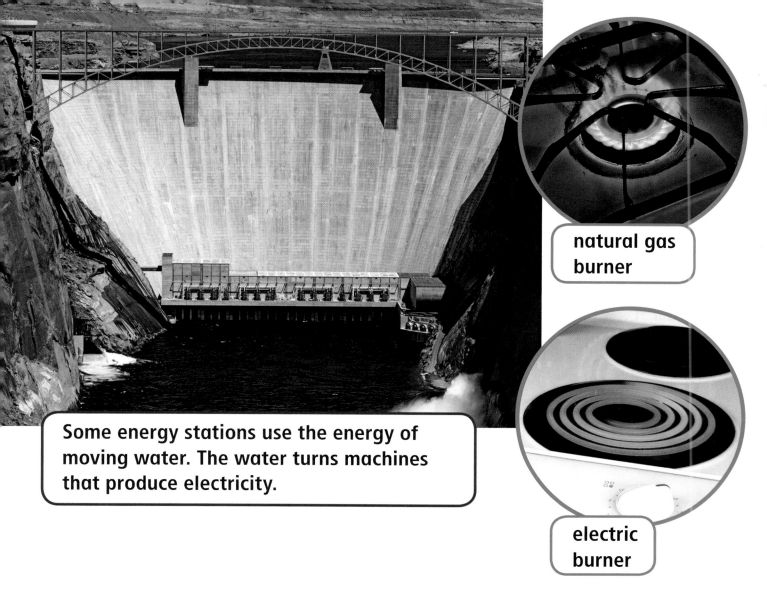

natural gas burner

electric burner

Some energy stations use the energy of moving water. The water turns machines that produce electricity.

Energy also comes from fuels, such as coal and oil. Gasoline is a fuel made from oil. Most cars use energy from gasoline to move. Some people use natural gas fuel to heat their homes and cook their food.

 MAIN IDEA AND DETAILS

Where does energy come from?

Insta-Lab

Water Power

Place three small objects in the middle of a pan. Pour some water into the pan at one end. Observe what happens to the objects.

Electricity

Electricity is a form of energy. People produce electricity by using energy from other sources, such as wind or coal. Electricity provides power for many of the things you use each day. These things change electricity into heat, light, sound, and other forms of energy. Electricity moves from outlets, through plugs and wires, into these things.

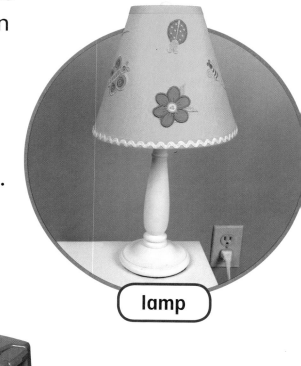

lamp

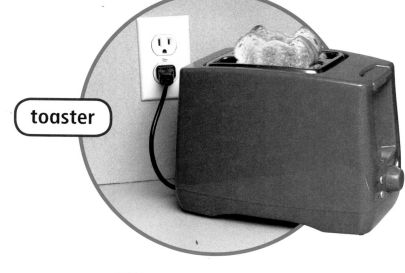

toaster

clock radio

outlet

The flashlight and other things below need electricity to work. But you do not plug them into outlets. Instead, you put batteries inside them.

Batteries store energy and change it to electricity. Batteries come in different shapes and sizes. Some have more energy than others.

Car Battery

MAIN IDEA AND DETAILS

What kinds of energy can electricity be changed into?

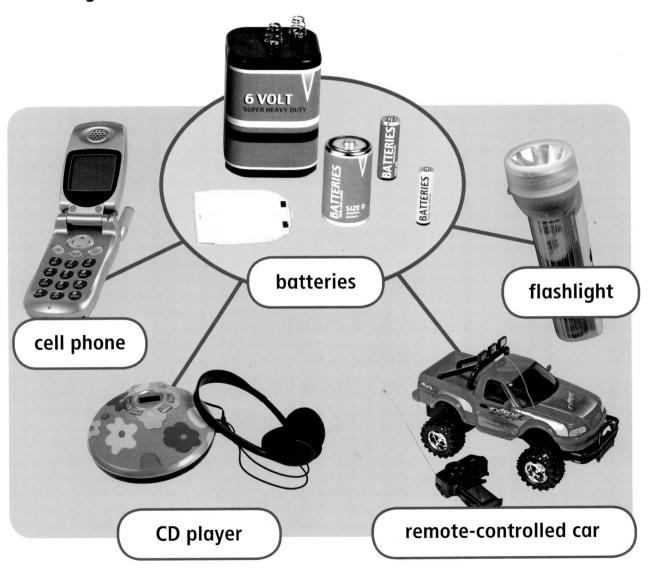

batteries

flashlight

cell phone

CD player

remote-controlled car

Electric Circuit

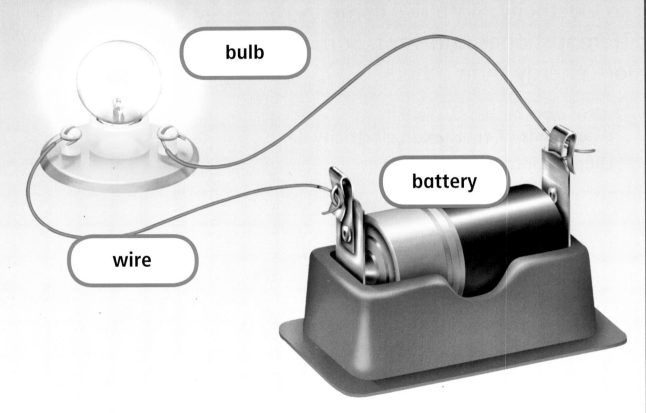

bulb

battery

wire

Electricity can travel in a path with ends that meet. This path is called a circuit.

A battery is the source of the electricity in this circuit. The electricity flows from the battery through the wires. The bulb will not light up if there are any gaps, or breaks, in the circuit.

For more links and animations, go to **www.hspscience.com**

Essential Question

What is energy?

In this lesson, you learned about energy, where it comes from, and how it can be used.

1. **Focus Skill** **MAIN IDEA AND DETAILS**
Make a chart like this one. Fill in details about this main idea. **Energy is something that can cause matter to move or change.**

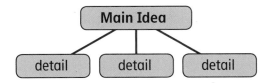

2. **VOCABULARY** Use the term **electricity** to tell about this picture.

3. **DRAW CONCLUSIONS** If you had an electric circuit and the bulb was not lit, what might you think was wrong?

4. **SUMMARIZE** Write a summary of this lesson. Begin with **Energy has.**

Test Prep

5. How does heat change things?
   A It makes them colder.
   B It makes them warmer.
   C It makes them slower.
   D It makes them smaller.

Make Connections

 Writing

Electricity Chart
Look around the classroom. Which things get electricity from batteries? Which things get electricity through an outlet? Make a chart to show your observations. Compare your chart with your classmates' charts.

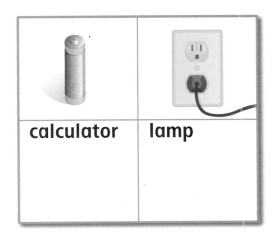

calculator	lamp

Investigate to find out how light moves.

Read and Learn about light.

Essential Question

What Is Light?

Fast Fact

Making Shadows

Light moves in straight lines. When something stops light from moving forward, the thing causes a shadow. You can draw conclusions about the way light moves.

448

To **reflect** is to bounce off. Light reflects when it hits most objects.
(p. 453)

How Light Moves

Guided Inquiry

Ask a Question

If you move the lamp, what will happen to the shadow? Investigate to find out. Then read and learn to find out more.

Get Ready

Inquiry Skill Tip
Use your observations and what you know to draw conclusions.

You need

small mirror

flashlight

What to Do

Step ①

Choose a spot on the wall on which you want light to shine. Then hold up the mirror.

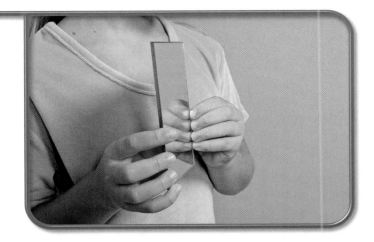

Step ②

Have a partner shine the flashlight onto the mirror.

Step ③

Move the mirror so that light shines onto the spot you chose.

Draw Conclusions

Draw conclusions about the way light moves.

Independent Inquiry

When you **draw conclusions**, you use your observations and what you know. Draw conclusions about how light will move if you use more than one mirror.

VOCABULARY
reflect

 **MAIN IDEA AND DETAILS**
Look for details about how light moves.

Light

Light is a form of energy that lets you see. Most light seems to have no color, but it actually can be made up of many colors.

You can see the colors in light when you look at a rainbow. A rainbow forms when sunlight passes through drops of water in the air. The water splits the light into all of its colors. What colors do you see in the rainbow?

> A glass prism acts like drops of water in the air. It splits the light into all of its colors.

rainbow

Light travels in straight lines. A flashlight shines light toward the spot at which you point it.

When light hits most objects, the objects **reflect**, or bounce, the light. You can see objects because they reflect light. Different objects reflect different amounts of light. A white, smooth surface reflects more light than a dark, rough one. Most mirrors are smooth and flat. They reflect most of the light that hits them.

Focus Skill **MAIN IDEA AND DETAILS**

How does light move?

Shadows

Light can pass through some objects but not others. An object that blocks light makes a shadow. When trees block sunlight, they make shadows on the ground.

Look at the picture of the people in the room. Light can pass through the glass windows. What is blocking the light? How can you tell?

MAIN IDEA AND DETAILS

What makes a shadow?

Insta-Lab

What Does Light Shine Through?

Shine a flashlight onto different materials. You might try wax paper, plastic wrap, newspaper, and construction paper. Which ones does light pass through? Communicate your results.

Essential Question

What is light?

In this lesson, you learned about light, reflection, and shadows.

1. **MAIN IDEA AND DETAILS**
Make a chart like this one.
Fill in details about this main
idea. **Light is a form of
energy.**

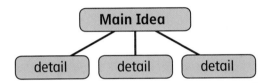

2. **VOCABULARY** Use the term
reflect to tell about light.

3. **DRAW CONCLUSIONS** How
can you tell if light cannot
pass through an object?

4. **SUMMARIZE** Use the chart to
write about the different ways
light is used.

Test Prep

5. Why do only some objects
make shadows?

Make Connections

 Math

Measure Shadows

Stand a pencil in a piece of clay. Put
it in a sunny place. Measure its shadow.
Record in a chart the time and the
shadow's length. Wait one hour.
Measure the shadow again, and record
its length. Repeat one hour later.

A Pencil's Shadow

time	length of shadow
9:00	5 inches
10:00	4 inches
11:00	3 inches

455

Investigate to find out about color and heat.

Read and Learn about heat.

Essential Question

What Is Heat?

Fast Fact

Color and Heat
Some colors absorb, or take in, more heat than others. This makes objects of some colors get warmer than objects of other colors. You can measure to find out which of two colors makes objects get warmer.

The coat of the darker horse will get hotter.

456

Friction is a force that slows down objects when they rub against each other. Friction also causes the objects to get warmer. (p. 460)

Temperature is the measure of how hot or cold something is. (p. 466)

Thermometer is a tool that measures an object's temperature. (p. 466)

Color and Heat

Ask a Question

Which of these two cars will get hotter?

Investigate to find out. Then read and learn to find out more.

Get Ready

Inquiry Skill Tip

You can use a thermometer to measure temperature.

You need

2 cups water

2 thermometers

black and white paper

tape

What to Do

Step 1

Fill each cup halfway with water. Place a thermometer in each cup.

Step 2

Tape black paper around the outside of one cup. Tape white paper around the other cup. Put both cups in a sunny place.

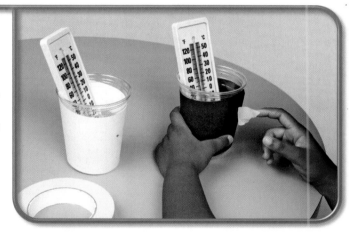

Step 3

After 30 minutes, **measure** the temperature of the water in each cup.

Draw Conclusions

Which temperature is higher? Why do you think that is?

Independent Inquiry

When you **measure** heat, you can use a thermometer. Measure heat in cups of water covered by paper of different colors.

VOCABULARY
friction
temperature
thermometer

 MAIN IDEA AND DETAILS
Look for details about how heat moves and how it is measured.

Heat and Burning

Heat is a form of energy that makes things warmer. In the daytime, you can feel heat that comes from the sun. The sun's heat warms land, water, air, and living things.

Objects can produce heat when they rub against each other. This heat comes from friction. **Friction** is a force that slows down objects that rub against each other. It also causes the objects to get warmer.

People also produce heat by burning fuel. Oil, natural gas, and wood are some fuels. The fuels give off heat as they burn.

Rubbing your hands together warms them.

forest fire

gas grill

oil lantern

Many people burn oil and natural gas to warm homes, schools, and other buildings. Natural gas is also used to cook food. As the gas burns, it gives off heat, which cooks the food.

Wood, from trees, burns very easily. Trees in forests can catch fire if people are not careful. Some people also burn wood in fireplaces to warm their homes.

Focus Skill **MAIN IDEA AND DETAILS**
How can people produce heat?

Insta-Lab

Making Heat
How do your hands feel? Are they warm or cool? Rub them together for 20 seconds. Then tell how they feel and how they changed.

461

Heat and Electricity

Many energy stations use heat to produce electricity. Heat changes water into steam, which turns machines that produce electricity. During this process, some heat is lost. It goes into the air or water.

Electricity moves from the energy station through power lines, or thick wires. The power lines carry electricity to homes, schools, and other buildings.

nuclear energy station

power lines

Electricity flows through wires in the walls, floors, and ceilings. Many wires go to outlets.

Electricity then flows to lamps and other objects that are plugged into outlets. These objects change the electricity to heat, light, or sound. An electric stove, for example, changes electricity to heat. Then the heat cooks food.

MAIN IDEA AND DETAILS

How do energy stations produce electricity?

How Heat Moves

Heat moves from warmer objects to cooler ones. When someone warms up cold stew, heat moves from the stove's burner to the pot. Then it moves from the pot to the cold stew. As the heat moves, the stew becomes warm.

Heat moves more easily and quickly through some things than others. Heat moves easily through metal. The metal spoon in the stew will get hot right away. Heat does not move as easily through plastic or wood.

wooden spoon

plastic spoon

metal spoon

Heat from an oven can make metal pots, pans, and trays very hot. People can burn their hands if they touch the metal. To protect their hands, people wear oven mitts.

Oven mitts are made from a thick material. Heat cannot move easily through it. A person who is using mitts can move a hot tray and not get burned. Most of the heat from the tray cannot get to the person's hands.

 **MAIN IDEA AND DETAILS**

How does heat move?

Temperature

Temperature is a measure of how hot or cold something is. A **thermometer** is a tool that measures an object's temperature. You can measure the temperature of air, food, and even your body. Temperature can be measured in degrees Fahrenheit and degrees Celsius.

Things that are hot have high temperatures. Things that are cold have low temperatures. Fire has a high temperature. Ice has a low temperature.

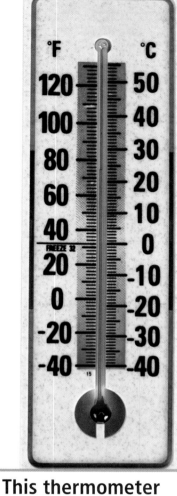

This thermometer shows temperature in degrees Fahrenheit and degrees Celsius.

MAIN IDEA AND DETAILS

Why do people use thermometers?

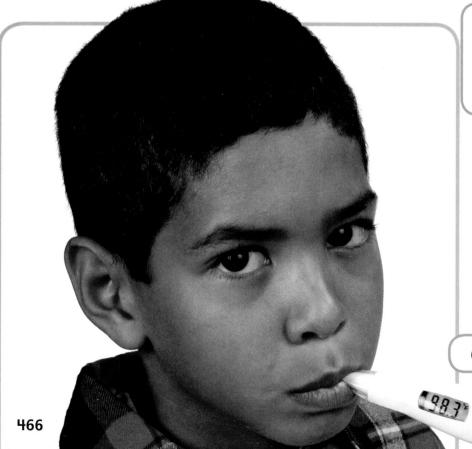

digital thermometer

Essential Question

What is heat?

In this lesson, you learned about heat, how heat moves, and some ways heat is used.

1. 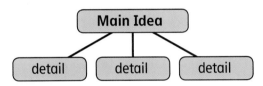 **MAIN IDEA AND DETAILS** Make a chart like this one. Fill in details about this main idea. **Heat is a form of energy that makes things warmer.**

```
              Main Idea
         /        |        \
    detail     detail     detail
```

2. VOCABULARY Use the terms **friction** and **heat** to tell about this picture.

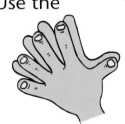

3. DRAW CONCLUSIONS If you had a hot tray of cookies, would you put the tray directly on the counter?

4. SUMMARIZE Use the chart to write a lesson summary.

Test Prep

5. What can you use to measure temperature?
   A friction
   B fireplace
   C thermometer
   D wires

Make Connections

 Math

Measure Temperatures
Fill a cup with cold water. Use a thermometer to measure the temperature of the water. Set the cup in a pan of warm water. After five minutes, measure the temperature again. How did it change? Why? Share your results.

James Joule

James Joule was a scientist who lived more than 180 years ago. He studied many things, but he was especially interested in electricity. He found that electricity produces heat.

In his research, Joule came up with an idea about heat and electricity that is now called Joule's law. It helps people figure out how much heat will be produced when electricity is used.

▶ **JAMES JOULE**
▶ Studied electricity

✏️ Think and Write

How does your family use heat from electricity?

Maria Telkes

► **DR. MARIA TELKES**

► Chemist and inventor

Think of all the energy the sun produces. What if people could catch this energy and use it to do things such as heat their homes and cook their food? Dr. Maria Telkes set out to find ways to do just that.

Maria Telkes was born in Hungary. She became interested in the power of the sun in high school. After finishing college, she moved to the United States. Then she began her work with solar energy. Dr. Telkes invented a solar oven to cook food and a solar heating system to keep homes warm. Her work went so well that many people called her the "Sun Queen."

 Think and Write

Dr. Telkes was a pioneer in her work, which means that she was one of the first. Do you think that solar energy will become more or less important in the future? Explain your answer.

Vocabulary Review

Use the terms to complete the sentences. The page numbers tell you where to look if you need help.

energy p. 440   **friction** p. 460

solar energy p. 442   **thermometer** p. 466

1. Energy from the sun is _____.

2. A force that slows down objects that rub against each other is _____.

3. Something that can cause movement or change is _____.

4. A tool that measures temperature is a _____.

Check Understanding

5. What are two ways to produce heat?

6. Why do these pots and pans have plastic handles?

7. Which of these is a
(Focus Skill) correct detail?

    A Friction is a form of energy.

    B Sound is a form of energy.

    C A shadow is a form of energy.

    D Color is a form of energy.

8. Why do trees make shadows?

    F Light is made up of many colors.

    G Light can not pass through trees.

    H Light can pass through trees.

    J Light comes from the sun.

Critical Thinking

9. Why do people sometimes use electricity from batteries instead of from outlets?

10. What energy does the sun provide to Earth?

The **Big Idea**

What's the Big Idea?

Sound can travel and is caused by vibrations.

Essential Questions

Student eBook
www.hspscience.com

Why can people who are far away from this train hear the sounds it makes? How does this connect to the **Big Idea?**

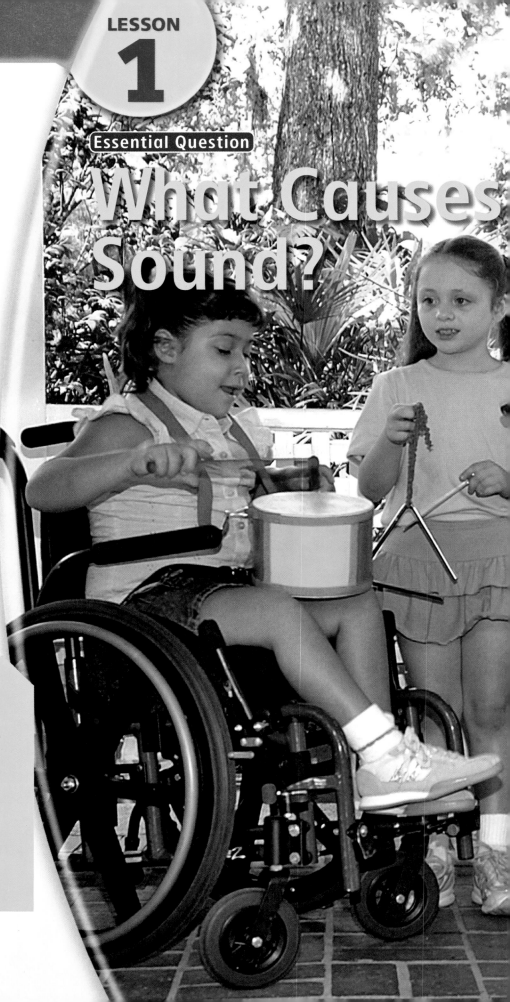

Investigate to find out how sound is made.

Read and Learn about what causes sound.

What Causes Sound?

Fast Fact

Making Sound
You can hear sounds all around you. Sometimes, you can feel sounds, too. You can communicate what you observe about sound.

Sound is energy you can hear. Sounds are made when an object vibrates. (p. 478)

To **vibrate** is to move back and forth quickly. (p. 478)

How Sound Is Made

Ask a Question

What are these children doing that causes the instruments to make sounds?

Investigate to find out. Then read and learn to find out more.

Get Ready

Inquiry Skill Tip

When you communicate, you share your ideas through writing, drawing, or speaking.

You need

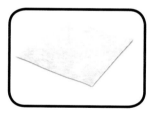

wax paper

tube with holes

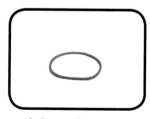

rubber band

What to Do

Step 1

Put wax paper over one end of a tube. Use a rubber band to hold the wax paper in place.

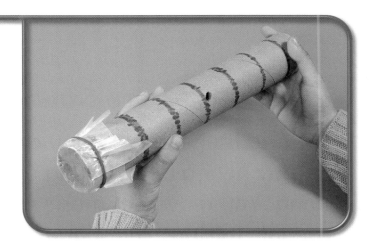

Step 2

Hum into the open end of the tube. What do you hear? Feel the wax paper. What do you feel? Stop humming. What changed?

Step 3

Communicate your observations to a classmate.

Draw Conclusions

Will the wax paper feel different if you hum louder?

Independent Inquiry

When you **communicate**, you share your ideas through writing, drawing, or speaking. Communicate your ideas about how different sounds are made.

Vibrations Make Sound

Sound is energy that you can hear. You may hear a dog barking or a bell ringing. You may hear music playing or people talking. The sounds are different, but they are made in the same way. All sound is made when something **vibrates**, or moves quickly back and forth.

> What things in these pictures are making sounds?

What things in these pictures are making sounds?

Objects make sounds when they vibrate. The top of a drum vibrates when you hit it. A guitar string vibrates when you pluck it. The vibrations make sounds. When the vibrations stop, the sounds stop. Some things, such as a drum or thunder, make sounds so loud that you can feel them, too.

 **CAUSE AND EFFECT**
What causes sound?

Make Vibrations
Hold a ruler on a desk so that one end hangs over the edge. Push that end down, and then let it go. What do you see, hear, and feel?

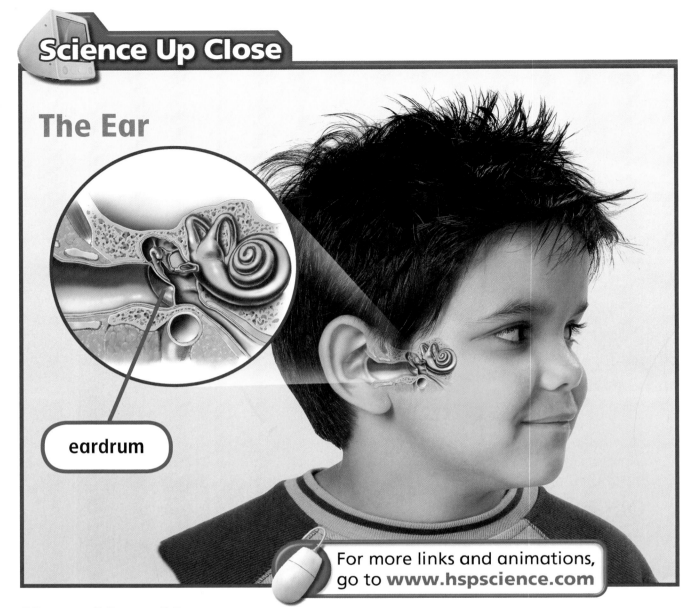

The Ear

eardrum

For more links and animations,
go to **www.hspscience.com**

How You Hear

You hear sounds with your ears. Sound
vibrations move through the air into your
ear. They move from your outer ear to your
inner ear. The vibrations cause the eardrum
and the tiny bones in your ear to vibrate.
The inner ear sends signals to the brain.
You hear a sound.

 **CAUSE AND EFFECT**

What causes you to hear a sound?

What causes sound?

In this lesson, you learned about sound, about vibration, and about how vibration causes sound.

1. (Focus Skill) **CAUSE AND EFFECT**
Make a chart like this one. Tell what the effects are when something vibrates, when something stops vibrating, and when vibrations move through the ear.

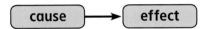

2. VOCABULARY Use the terms **vibrate** and **sound** to tell how sound is made.

3. DRAW CONCLUSIONS If you cover your ears, can you hear sounds as well as you can when your ears are uncovered?

4. SUMMARIZE Write two sentences that tell what this lesson is about.

Test Prep

5. What happens when a guitar string stops vibrating?

    A The sound gets louder.

    B The sound stops.

    C The eardrum vibrates.

    D The sound gets softer.

Make Connections

 Writing

Description of Sounds
Sit quietly, and listen to the sounds around you. Then write about the sounds you hear. Describe the way they sound.

I hear a door squeak.

A dog barks outside.

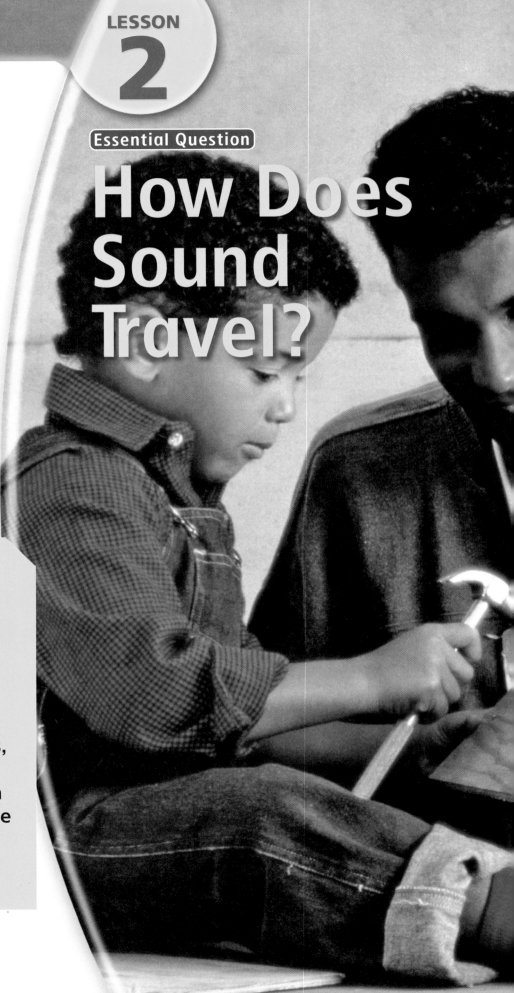

Investigate to find out about how sound travels.

Read and Learn about sound's traveling.

Essential Question

How Does Sound Travel?

Fast Fact

Sound Travels Through Wood

Most sound you hear travels through air to reach your ears. Sound can also travel through solids, such as wood, and through liquids, such as water. You can use what you know to predict how a sound will travel.

A **sound wave** is a vibration moving through matter. When sound waves reach your ears, you can hear sound. (p. 486)

How Sound Travels

Guided Inquiry

Ask a Question

Can you hear sirens from far away?
Investigate to find out. Then read and learn to find out more.

Get Ready

Inquiry Skill Tip
To predict, think about what you already know and then tell what you think will happen.

You need

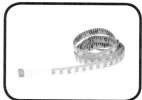

tape measure

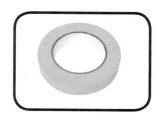

masking tape

What to Do

Step ❶

Use the tape measure to measure 50 centimeters on your desk. Mark each end with tape.

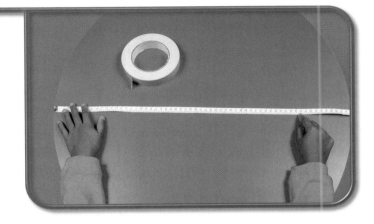

Step ❷

Scratch at one tape mark and listen at the other. **Predict** whether you will hear the sound if you put your ear on the desk. Try it.

Step ❸

What did you observe?

Draw Conclusions

Was your **prediction** correct?

Independent Inquiry

To **predict**, think about what you already know and then tell what you think will happen. Look around your classroom and make other predictions about how sound travels.

VOCABULARY
sound wave

MAIN IDEA AND DETAILS

Look for the different kinds of matter that sound can travel through.

Sound Travels Through Air

Sound can travel through different kinds of matter. Sound can travel through gases, such as air. When an object vibrates, it produces sound waves. **Sound waves** are vibrations that are moving through matter. The sound waves travel through the air to your ears, and you hear the sound.

486

Sound moves in all directions. When a rooster crows, people all around the rooster can hear it.

Sound waves can be blocked. Some people use ear coverings to protect their ears from loud sounds. This keeps some of the sound waves from reaching their eardrums.

 **MAIN IDEA AND DETAILS**
How does sound move?

Sound Travels Through Water

Sound travels through liquids, such as water. Sound travels faster through water than through air.

Dolphins make sounds to find things underwater. The sounds travel through the water. When they hit objects, they bounce off. The bounced sounds are called echoes. The dolphins listen to the echoes to tell how far away things are.

Sound waves from the tuning fork move through the water. They make the water vibrate.

dolphin

humpback whales

Humpback whales also make sounds underwater. Their sounds are like songs. The whales may sing for many hours at a time. Their songs can reach other whales that are far away.

 **MAIN IDEA AND DETAILS**
What is one liquid that sound can travel through?

Make Waves
Fill a cup with water. Gently touch the water with a pencil eraser. What do you see? Tell a classmate how the ripples are moving. How are these little waves like sound waves?

Sound Travels Through Solids

Sound travels through solids, such as wood and glass. Sound travels faster through most solids than through gases or liquids.

Have you ever talked on a string telephone? A string connects two cans. One person talks into a can. The sound waves make the air in the can vibrate. This makes the can vibrate, and then the can makes the string vibrate.

The sound waves travel through the string and make the other can and the air in it vibrate. The vibrations travel into that person's ear, and he or she hears the sound.

MAIN IDEA AND DETAILS

In a string telephone, how does sound travel from one can to the other?

Essential Question

How does sound travel?

In this lesson, you learned about how sound travels through air, water, and solids.

1. 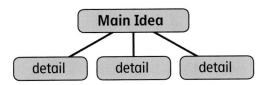 **MAIN IDEA AND DETAILS** Make a chart like this one. Fill in details about this main idea. **Sound travels through different kinds of matter.**

```
          Main Idea
         /    |    \
   detail  detail  detail
```

2. VOCABULARY Use the term **sound waves** to tell about the picture.

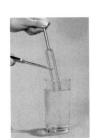

3. DRAW CONCLUSIONS How can you tell that sound travels in all directions?

4. SUMMARIZE Use the chart to tell what you learned about sound and how it travels.

Test Prep

5. Which kind of matter does sound travel through the fastest?
   A solids
   B liquids
   C gases
   D liquids and gases

Make Connections

 **Math**

Order from Least to Greatest
Sound travels at different speeds through different kinds of matter. Order the speeds in the chart from slowest to fastest.

Speed of Sound in Meters per Second

kind of matter	speed
water	1,433
glass	5,030
air	343
gold	3,240
rubber	1,600

How Do We Make Different Sounds?

Investigate to find out why sounds are different.

Read and Learn about how to make different sounds.

Fast Fact

Loud or Soft Sound

Guitar strings make different sounds because they are not all the same. Some are thick. Some are thin. Some are tighter than others. You can hypothesize why sounds are different.

492

Vocabulary Preview

Loudness is how loud or soft a sound is. (p.496)

Pitch is how high or low a sound is. (p. 498)

493

Why Sounds Are Different

Guided Inquiry

Ask a Question

These drums make different sounds. What makes them sound different?

Investigate to find out. Then read and learn to find out more.

Get Ready

You need

colored water

3 glasses

wooden spoon

What to Do

Step ①

Pour a different amount of water into each glass. **Hypothesize** whether all the glasses will sound the same when you tap them.

Step ②

Use the spoon to tap each glass on the side. Was your **hypothesis** correct?

Step ③

Find a way to make all the glasses sound the same.

Draw Conclusions

Would changing the amount of water change the sound?

Independent Inquiry

When you **hypothesize**, you make an explanation that you can test. Hypothesize whether different liquids will sound the same when you tap them.

VOCABULARY
loudness
pitch

CAUSE AND EFFECT

Look for what causes different sounds.

Loud or Soft

Sounds are different. They may be loud or soft. A shout is a loud sound. A whisper is a soft, or quiet, sound.

The **loudness** of a sound is how loud or soft it is. It takes more energy to make a loud sound than a soft sound.

The closer you are to what makes a sound, the louder the sound you hear. It's hard to hear people talk when you are far away from them. As you move closer, you can hear them more easily.

 CAUSE AND EFFECT

What happens when a lot of energy is used to make a sound?

Loud and Soft

Clap as loudly as you can. Then clap as softly as you can. Does it take more energy to clap loudly or to clap softly?

High or Low

Sounds are also different in **pitch**, or how high or low they are. A whistle makes a sound with a high pitch. A big drum makes a sound with a low pitch.

The speed of an object's vibration makes its sound's pitch low or high. Thicker or longer strings vibrate more slowly. They make a sound with a low pitch. Thinner or shorter strings vibrate faster. They make a sound with a high pitch.

(Focus Skill) **CAUSE AND EFFECT**

What makes a sound's pitch high or low?

A xylophone has long and short bars. The long bars make sounds with low pitches. The short bars make sounds with high pitches.

Essential Question

How do we make different sounds?

In this lesson, you learned how different sounds are made.

1. 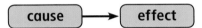 **CAUSE AND EFFECT** Make a chart like this one. Tell what sounds are the effects of a lot of energy and a little energy being used. Then tell the effects of quick and slow vibrations.

cause → effect

2. **VOCABULARY** Explain the meaning of the terms **loudness** and **pitch**.

3. **DRAW CONCLUSIONS** Suppose you wanted to make a string instrument that made both high-pitched and low-pitched sounds. What kinds of strings would you use?

4. **SUMMARIZE** Write a summary of this lesson. Begin with the sentence **Sounds can be different**.

Test Prep

5. What happens when a string vibrates very quickly?

   A It makes a high sound.
   B It makes a low sound.
   C It makes no sound.
   D It makes a soft sound.

Make Connections

 Social Studies

Too Many Sounds
Too many sounds can cause noise pollution. Make a list of problems caused by too much sound. Then, for each sound problem, write a way people could solve it.

Noise Pollution

problem	solution
The radio and television are both on.	Turn one off.

Alexander Graham Bell

▶ **ALEXANDER GRAHAM BELL**
▶ Inventor

Alexander Graham Bell was an inventor. He worked on inventing machines that used sound. He wanted to help people who could not hear.

Alexander Graham Bell made a discovery. He found that he could send speech sounds over an electric wire. He used his discovery to patent something that is still very important today—the telephone!

 Think and Write

How did Alexander Graham Bell's work with sound change people's lives?

model of a telephone

▶ **AMAR BOSE**
▶ Engineer
▶ Inventor

Amar Bose

Amar Bose was disappointed that the music from his stereo did not sound as good as music at a live concert. He decided to build a stereo that produced better sound.

Amar Bose researched the way people hear sounds. He used this information to make a new kind of stereo speakers. The music from these speakers sounded much more like live music.

In a concert hall, most of the sound bounces from the stage to the walls and ceilings. Then it goes to a person's ear. Bose made his speakers so that they directed sound in much the same way. These speakers have improved the way music sounds in homes, cars, theaters, and even in Olympic stadiums.

Think and Write
Many inventions solve a problem. What problem did Bose's invention solve?

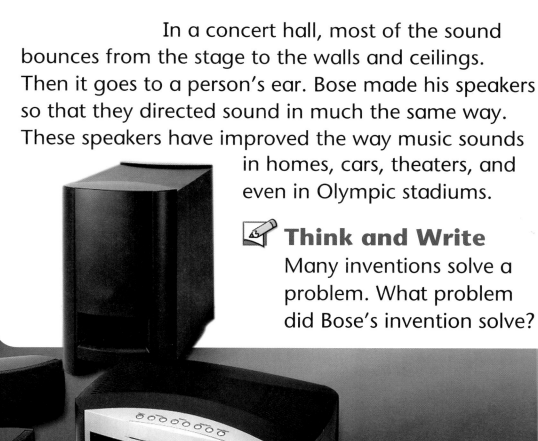

Vocabulary Review

Use the terms below to complete the sentences. The page numbers tell you where to look if you need help.

sound p. 478   **sound waves** p. 486

vibrate p. 478   **pitch** p. 498

1. When guitar strings move back and forth, they _____.

2. Energy that you can hear is _____.

3. The highness or lowness of a sound is its _____.

4. Vibrations that move through matter are _____.

Check Understanding

5. What causes the sound a drum makes?

   A ears
   B loudness
   C pitch
   D vibrations

6. What can sound move through?

  F only air and water

  G only air and solids

  H only water and solids

  J air, water, and solids

Critical Thinking

7. Does it take more energy to whisper or to shout? Explain.

8. Tell how ears can hear the sounds of a harp.

The **Big Idea**

What's the **Big Idea?**

We can observe and measure the ways things move.

Essential Questions

Lesson 1

What Are Ways Things Move?

Lesson 2

What Makes Things Move?

Lesson 3

How Do Magnets Move Things?

Go online

Student eBook
www.hspscience.com

504

Will this sled move faster when it goes up the hill or when it goes down the hill? How does this connect to the **Big Idea?**

505

Essential Question

What Are Ways Things Move?

Investigate to find out about how things can move.

Read and Learn about ways in which things can move.

Fast Fact

Rolling Motion
A rolling ball will move in a straight line if it is not touched. You can plan an investigation to find different ways a ball can move.

Motion is movement. When something moves, it is in motion. (p. 510)

Speed is how fast something moves. (p. 512)

How Things Can Move

Guided Inquiry

Ask a Question

In what direction does the bowler want his ball to travel? Investigate to find out. Then read and learn to find out more.

Get Ready

Inquiry Skill Tip
When you plan an investigation, you think of a way to find an answer to a question.

You need

golf ball

classroom objects

What to Do

Step ❶

Roll the ball in a straight line.

Step ❷

In how many different ways can you make the ball move? **Plan an investigation** to find out. Use classroom objects to help you.

Step ❸

Follow your plan. Communicate your observations.

Draw Conclusions

What might happen if the ball hits an object?

Independent Inquiry

Plan an investigation to find out how things move downhill.

VOCABULARY
motion
speed

Look for details about the ways things can move.

Kinds of Motion

When something moves, it is in **motion**. A ball is in motion when it is rolling.

Objects can move in many paths. A toy car can move in a straight line. A swing moves back and forth in a curved path. The hands of a clock move in a circle. A bike moves in a curved path when it turns a corner. A ball curves and may zigzag up and down as it bounces.

How are objects moving in this picture?

MAIN IDEA AND DETAILS
What are some different ways an object can move?

straight

YOU PUTT GOLF

back and forth

circle

curve

zigzag

511

Fast and Slow

Speed describes how fast something moves. Things move at different speeds. A car can move faster than a bike. A skater can move faster than a person who is walking.

Focus Skill MAIN IDEA AND DETAILS

What do the words <u>fast</u> and <u>slow</u> describe?

Insta-Lab

Watch It Go!

Write a list of things that can go fast. Exchange lists with a partner. How many things did you and your partner write on your lists?

Essential Question

What are ways things move?

In this lesson, you learned about kinds of motion, including fast and slow.

1. 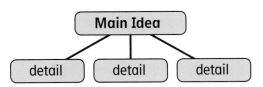 **MAIN IDEA AND DETAILS**
Make a chart like this one. Fill in details about this main idea. **Objects can move in different paths and at different speeds.**

```
      Main Idea
    /     |     \
 detail detail detail
```

2. VOCABULARY
Explain the meanings of the terms **motion** and **speed**.

3. DRAW CONCLUSIONS
Suppose an object is moving straight. How could you make it move back and forth instead?

4. SUMMARIZE Write two sentences that tell what this lesson is about.

Test Prep
5. What are some different ways things can move?

Make Connections

 Writing

Description of Ways Things Move
Look at things outside that move. Write sentences that tell about the direction and speed of the moving objects.

I see a plane flying in a straight line. It is moving very fast.

Investigate to find out about how to move objects.

Read and Learn about what makes things move.

Essential Question

What Makes Things Move?

Fast Fact

Paddling Motion

A person moves a kayak by pulling one end of the paddle and then the other. You can classify the way you move an object as a push or a pull.

A **force** is a push or a pull that makes something move. Magnetism is one kind of force. (p. 518)

Gravity is a force that pulls things toward the center of Earth. (p. 520)

Friction is a force that slows down objects when they rub against each other. Friction also causes the objects to get warmer. (p. 521)

A **lever** is a simple machine made up of a bar that pivots, or turns on a fixed point. (p. 522)

An **inclined plane** is a simple machine that makes it easier to move or lift things. (p. 523)

Use a Lever

Guided Inquiry

Ask a Question

This person is using a lever to open the paint can. Do you see the lever?

Investigate to find out. Then read and learn to find out more.

Get Ready

Inquiry Skill Tip

You can make a model of a simple lever to find out how it works.

You need

2 chalkboard erasers

rigid meterstick

small, thin book

What to Do

Step ①

Stack two chalkboard erasers to **make a model**.

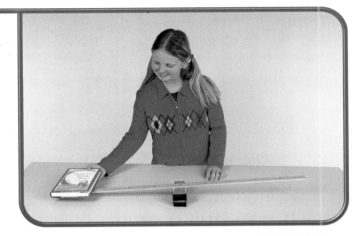

Step ②

Put the meterstick on top of the erasers. Put the book at one end of the meterstick.

Step ③

Press down on one end of the meterstick. Watch what happens to the book.

Draw Conclusions

How did using the meterstick and erasers make lifting the book easier?

Independent Inquiry

Can you **make a model** of a lever with other classroom objects? Use books, magazines, or other objects to make a lever. Try to move something. Was the object easier to move?

VOCABULARY
force
gravity
friction

CAUSE AND EFFECT
Look for the causes of motion.

Forces and Motion

A **force** is a push or a pull. You can use pushes and pulls to change where an object is. If you push a swing, it moves away from you. If you pull a swing, it moves toward you.

You can use force to change the direction of a moving object. When you kick a ball, you push it. A push on the right-hand side of the ball will make it go to the left. A push on the left-hand side will make it go to the right.

pull

push

The more force you use, the farther and faster an object will move. A strong kick will push a ball farther and faster than a gentle kick. You need a small force to move a light ball quickly. You need more force to move a heavy ball just as quickly.

CAUSE AND EFFECT

What causes objects to move?

Insta-Lab

More or Less?

Push a book gently across a table. Then push a pile of two or three books across the table. Did you use more or less force to move the pile than you used to move the single book?

Gravity

Gravity is a force that pulls things toward the center of Earth. It makes things fall unless something holds them up. When you let go of something, gravity causes it to fall to the ground. Gravity causes a ball to roll downhill. It pulls your body down a slide. Gravity keeps people on the ground, too.

CAUSE AND EFFECT
How does gravity cause objects to move?

Friction

Friction is a force that slows or stops things that are moving. This happens when two things rub against each other. A bike chain rubs against the gears. A rusty chain makes a bike harder to pedal.

Smooth surfaces cause less friction than rough ones. Smooth surfaces do not slow moving things as much. It is easier to ride a bike with a smooth, clean chain than a rusty one.

 **CAUSE AND EFFECT**
What effect does friction have on moving objects?

Levers

You can move things with the help of a simple machine called a **lever**.

A lever is a bar that sits on a turning point. Levers lessen the force needed to handle materials.

To understand how levers work, you need to think about three things—the turning point of the lever; the load, or the thing you are trying to move; and the force you apply.

Sometimes you push down on one end of the lever, and that causes the other end to move upward. Think about a shovel. Sometimes you pull up on the lever. That raises the load. Think about a wheelbarrow.

Focus Skill CAUSE AND EFFECT

What happens when you pull up on the tab of a soda can?

A shovel is a lever.

Inclined Plane

You can also move things using an **inclined plane**. An inclined plane is a slanting surface that joins a lower level to a higher level. Have you ever walked up stairs or gone down a slide? If so, you've used an inclined plane.

With an inclined plane, less force is needed to move objects. This makes the work easier. The load may have to go a longer distance, though. Think about pushing a heavy box up a ramp. It has to go a little farther, but it is much easier to move.

 **CAUSE AND EFFECT**

Why would someone want to use an inclined plane to move an object?

Bike Brakes

Bike brakes use friction to stop a bike. When you ride a bike, the brakes do not touch the wheels. There is no friction between them.

To stop the bike, you press the brakes against the wheels. The brakes rub against the wheels and cause friction. The wheels turn more and more slowly until they stop moving.

brakes off

brakes on

For more links and animations, go to **www.hspscience.com**

Essential Question

What makes things move?

In this lesson, you learned about forces and motion, gravity, friction, levers, and inclined planes.

1. 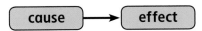 **CAUSE AND EFFECT**
Make a chart like this one. Tell what causes an object to move, an object to move toward Earth, or an object that is moving to slow or stop.

cause ⟶ effect

2. VOCABULARY How is **force** being used in the picture?

3. DRAW CONCLUSIONS Why does a skater on a rough surface slow down faster than one skating on a smooth surface?

4. SUMMARIZE Write three sentences to tell what this lesson is mostly about.

Test Prep

5. What causes a book to fall to the ground when you drop it?

   A friction

   B gravity

   C pushing

   D speed

Make Connections

 Math

Measure Motion

Roll a toy car down a ramp. Use a meterstick to measure how far the car moved after it reached the bottom. Record the distance in a chart. Place a towel over the ramp and repeat. Why is the second distance different from the first? What is the difference between the distances?

How Far a Car Moves

without a towel	2 meters
with a towel	

Investigate to find out how magnets work.

Read and Learn about how magnets move things.

Essential Question

How Do Magnets Move Things?

Fast Fact

Use a Magnet
Magnets can move some objects without touching them. You can hypothesize how magnets will move other magnets.

A **magnet** is an object that can pull things made of iron and steel. (p. 530)

A **pole** is an end of a magnet. All magnets have a north-seeking pole and a south-seeking pole. (p. 531)

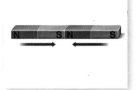

To **attract** something is to pull toward it. Opposite poles of two magnets attract each other. (p. 531)

To **repel** something is to push it away. Poles that are the same on two magnets repel each other. (p. 531)

How Magnets Work

Get Ready

Guided Inquiry

Ask a Question

What is making these things stay on the board? Investigate to find out. Then read and learn to find out more.

Inquiry Skill Tip

When you hypothesize, you make an explanation you can test.

You need

2 bar magnets

What to Do

Step ①

Hypothesize what will happen when you bring together the ends of two magnets.

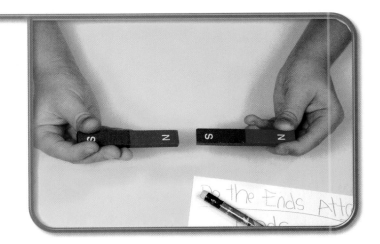

Step ②

Make a chart like this one.

Do the Ends Attract or Repel?

Ends	Attract or Repel
N end and S end	
N end and N end	
S end and S end	

Step ③

Bring the N end of one magnet toward the S end of the other one. Record what you observe. Repeat, using the two N ends and then the two S ends.

Draw Conclusions

Was your **hypothesis** correct?

Independent Inquiry

When you **hypothesize**, you make a statement you can test. Hypothesize how a paper clip will interact with a magnet.

VOCABULARY
magnet
pole
attract
repel

 MAIN IDEA AND DETAILS

Look for details about magnets.

Magnets

A **magnet** is an object that can pull things made of iron or steel. It can also push or pull other magnets. Many magnets are made of metal. Most of them are made by people. They come in many shapes and sizes. They may look like bars, horseshoes, balls, or rings.

Lodestone is a kind of rock that is a magnet. Lodestone is found in nature.

All magnets have two **poles**, or ends. One end is the north-seeking pole, or N pole. The other end is the south-seeking pole, or S pole.

Opposite poles **attract**, or pull, each other. The N pole of one magnet and the S pole of another magnet attract each other. The two N poles or the two S poles on different magnets **repel** each other, or push each other away.

 **MAIN IDEA AND DETAILS**   What are magnets?

Which two magnets attract each other? Which two repel each other?

Magnetic Attraction

Make a pile of small classroom objects. Test them with a magnet. Which ones does the magnet attract? How are those objects alike?

What Magnets Do

Magnets can pull iron and steel objects without touching them. They can also push and pull other magnets without touching them. Magnets can do this because their force can pass through air, water, and some solids.

The magnet below can pull the toy truck because the truck has iron in it. The magnet's force passes through the air, so the magnet pulls the truck without touching it.

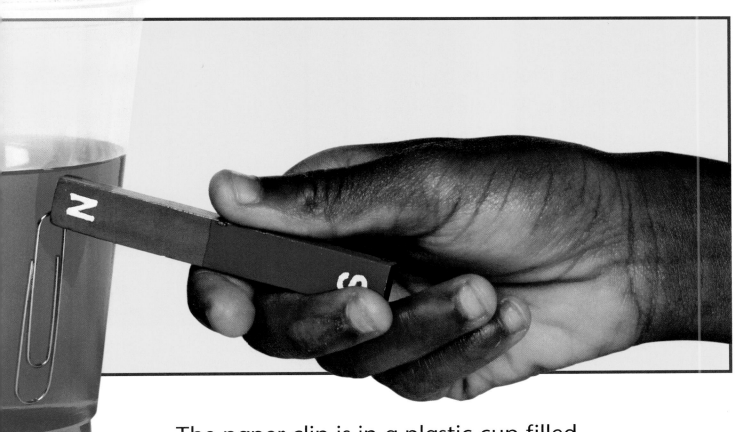

The paper clip is in a plastic cup filled with water. The magnet moved the paper clip from the bottom of the cup to the side of the cup without touching the paper clip. The pull of the magnet can pass through plastic and water.

Focus Skill) MAIN IDEA AND DETAILS

What can the force of a magnet pass through?

How People Use Magnets

People use magnets in many ways. They use magnets to hold things together and to lift things. Magnets can hold cabinet doors shut. They can hold things to surfaces made of iron or steel. Large magnets can help lift and move heavy metal objects, such as cars. Magnets are used in some doorbells and telephones.

(Focus Skill) **MAIN IDEA AND DETAILS**

How do people use magnets?

A can opener holds a can in place while the opener cuts off its lid. Then a magnet holds the lid while someone pulls away the can.

A compass magnet is shaped like a needle. It always points north.

A refrigerator magnet can hold up pieces of paper.

Essential Question

How do magnets move things?

In this lesson, you learned about magnets, what they can do, and ways people use them.

1. 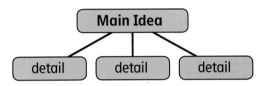 **MAIN IDEA AND DETAILS**
Make a chart like this one. Fill in details about this main idea. **Magnets can push and pull things made of iron or steel.**

```
        ┌──────────────┐
        │  Main Idea   │
        └──────────────┘
       /       |        \
 ┌────────┐ ┌────────┐ ┌────────┐
 │ detail │ │ detail │ │ detail │
 └────────┘ └────────┘ └────────┘
```

2. **VOCABULARY** Use the terms **magnet, poles,** and **attract** to tell about the picture.

3. **DRAW CONCLUSIONS** How could you find out if an object was made of iron or steel?

4. **SUMMARIZE** Use the chart to write a lesson summary.

Test Prep
5. How can magnets move objects?

Make Connections

 Art

Magnet Inventions

Invent a toy or a tool that uses a magnet. Draw a picture of it. Write a description of what it does and how to make it. Share your invention with the class.

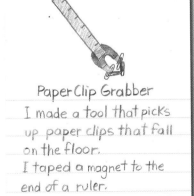

Paper Clip Grabber
I made a tool that picks up paper clips that fall on the floor.
I taped a magnet to the end of a ruler.

Swimmers Glide Like Sharks

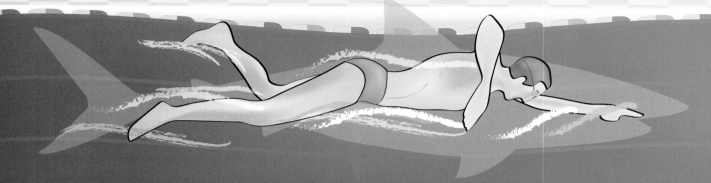

Scientists have invented a new swimsuit that helps Olympic athletes glide through the water. To make the suit, scientists turned to one of the best swimmers in nature, the shark. The new swimsuit, called Fastskin, looks and feels like a shark's skin.

SHARK'S SKIN SUIT

Sharks have tiny V-shaped ridges on their skin. The ridges turn water away from the shark so that the water does not slow down the fish.

Studying Sharks

To make Fastskin, scientists first studied a real shark's skin under a big magnifier. Then they copied the pattern of the skin on the new swimsuit. The Fastskin has the same kind of ridges that a real shark's skin has.

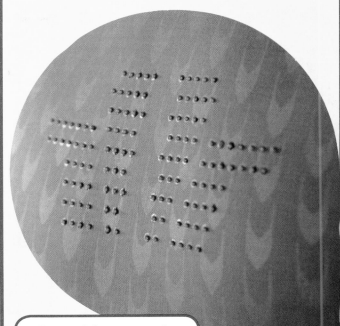

Fastskin sample

Fastskin helps swimmers move through the water by cutting down on turbulence. One kind of turbulence is stirred-up water, which can slow down swimmers. Fastskin is made of synthetic, or human-made, fabrics. The Fastskin suit is very tight and can take up to 15 minutes to squeeze into.

 Think and Write

How does less turbulence in the water help an Olympic swimmer?

Find out more. Log on to
www.hspscience.com

Vocabulary Review

Use the terms below to complete the sentences. The page numbers tell you where to look if you need help.

motion p. 510   **gravity** p. 520

speed p. 512   **inclined plane** p. 523

force p. 518   **magnet** p. 530

1. A force that pulls things toward the center of Earth is _____.

2. A slanting surface is an _____.

3. How fast something moves is its _____.

4. When something moves, it is in _____.

5. A push or a pull is a _____.

6. An object that can push or pull things that are made of iron or steel is a _____.

Check Understanding

7. Which spoon may a magnet be able to pull?

8. Mae hits a baseball lightly. Then she uses more force to hit the baseball. What effect does this have on the baseball?

   A The baseball moves more quickly.

   B The baseball moves more slowly.

   C The baseball does not move as far.

   D The baseball stops moving.

Critical Thinking

9. Why do you need gravity to swing?

10. Would a car travel slowly or fast on a road that is icy or wet?

The **Big Idea**

Visual Summary

Tell how each picture shows the **Big Idea** for its chapter.

CHAPTER 11 Big Idea

Light and heat are forms of energy.

CHAPTER 12 Big Idea

Sound can travel and is caused by vibrations.

CHAPTER 13 Big Idea

We can observe and measure the ways things move.

Visit the Multimedia Science Glossary to see illustrations of these words and to hear them pronounced. www.hspscience.com

Every entry in the glossary begins with a term and a *phonetic respelling*. A phonetic respelling writes the word the way it sounds, which can help you pronounce new or unfamiliar words. The definition of the term follows the respelling. An example of how to use the term in a sentence follows the definition.

If there is a page number in ( ) at the end of the entry, it tells you where to find the term in your textbook. These terms are highlighted in yellow in the chapter in your textbook. Each entry has an illustration to help you understand the term.

The Pronunciation Key below will help you understand the respellings. Syllables are separated by a bullet (•). Small, uppercase letters show stressed syllables.

Pronunciation Key

Sound	As in	Phonetic Respelling	Sound	As in	Phonetic Respelling
a	bat	(BAT)	oh	over	(OH•ver)
ah	lock	(LAHK)	oo	pool	(POOL)
air	rare	(RAIR)	ow	out	(OWT)
ar	argue	(AR•gyoo)	oy	foil	(FOYL)
aw	law	(LAW)	s	cell	(SEL)
ay	face	(FAYS)		sit	(SIT)
ch	chapel	(CHAP•uhl)	sh	sheep	(SHEEP)
e	test	(TEST)	th	that	(THAT)
	metric	(MEH•trik)		thin	(THIN)
ee	eat	(EET)	u	pull	(PUL)
	feet	(FEET)	uh	medal	(MED•uhl)
	ski	(SKEE)		talent	(TAL•uhnt)
er	paper	(PAY•per)		pencil	(PEN•suhl)
	fern	(FERN)		onion	(UHN•yuhn)
eye	idea	(eye•DEE•uh)		playful	(PLAY•fuhl)
i	bit	(BIT)		dull	(DUHL)
ing	going	(GOH•ing)	y	yes	(YES)
k	card	(KARD)		ripe	(RYP)
	kite	(KYT)	z	bags	(BAGZ)
ngk	bank	(BANGK)	zh	treasure	(TREZH•er)

Multimedia Science Glossary www.hspscience.com

adapt [uh•DAPT]

To change. Animals and plants adapt over time to live in their environments. (157)

amphibian [am•FIB•ee•uhn]

The group of animals with smooth, wet skin. Young amphibians live in the water, and most adults live on land. (96)

attract [uh•TRAKT]

To pull something. Opposite poles of two magnets attract each other. (531)

bird [BERD]

The group of animals with feathers on their bodies and wings. Most birds can fly. (86)

boulder [BOHL•der]

A very large rock. (210)

burning [BER•ning]

The change of a substance into ashes and smoke. (424)

C

centimeter [SEN•tuh•mee•ter]

A unit used to measure how long a solid is. Centimeters are marked on many rulers. (375)

condensation

[kahn•duhn•SAY•shuhn]

The change of water from a gas to a liquid. Condensation happens when heat is taken away from water vapor. (418)

condense [kuhn•DENS]

To change from water vapor gas into liquid water. Water vapor condenses when heat is taken away. (296)

constellation

[kahn•stuh•LAY•shuhn]

A group of stars that seems to form a pattern. (314)

D

desert [DEZ•ert]

An environment that is very dry because it gets little rain. (164)

dinosaur [DY•nuh•sawr]

An animal that lived on Earth millions of years ago. Dinosaurs have become extinct. (220)

drought [DROWT]

A long time when it does not rain. During a drought, the land may become dry, and plants may die. (298)

 E

earthquake [ERTH•kwayk]

A shaking of Earth's surface that can cause land to rise and fall. (202)

electricity
[uh•lek•TRIH•sih•tee]

A form of energy. People produce electricity by using energy from other sources. (444)

endangered [en•DAYN•jerd]

In danger of not being alive anymore. People can help endangered animals by protecting the places in which they live. (261)

energy [EN•er•jee]

Something that can cause matter to move or change. Heat, light, and sound are forms of energy. (440)

environment
[en•VY•ruhn•muhnt]

All the living and nonliving things in a place. (154)

erosion [uh•ROH•zhuhn]

A kind of change that happens when wind and water move sand and small rocks to a new place. (106)

evaporate [ee•VAP•uh•rayt]

To change from liquid water into a gas. Water evaporates when heat is added. (296)

evaporation
[ee•vap•uh•RAY•shuhn]

The change of water from a liquid to a gas. Evaporation happens when heat is added to liquid water. (417)

extinct [ek•STINGT]

No longer living. Dinosaurs are extinct because none of them live anymore. (220)

 F

fish [FISH]

The group of animals that live in water and get oxygen through gills. Fish have scales and use fins to swim. (97)

flowers [FLOW•erz]

The plant parts that help a plant make new plants. Part of the flower makes seeds that grow into new plants. (121)

food chain [FOOD CHAYN]

A diagram that shows the order in which animals eat other living things. (176)

food web [FOOD WEB]

A diagram that shows how food chains are connected. (178)

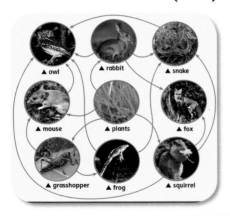

force [FAWRS]

A push or a pull that makes something move. Magnetism is one kind of force. (518)

fossil [FAHS•uhl]

What is left of an animal or a plant that lived long ago. A fossil can be a print in a rock or bones that have turned to rock. (220)

friction [FRIK•shuhn]

A force that slows down objects when they rub against each other. Friction also causes the objects to get warmer. (460, 521)

G

gas [GAS]

The only form of matter that always fills all the space of its container. (390)

germinate [JER•muh•nayt]

To start to grow. A seed may germinate when it gets water, warmth, and oxygen. (136)

grassland [GRAS•land]

An open environment covered with grass. (166)

gravity [GRAV•ih•tee]

A force that pulls things toward the center of Earth. (520)

 H

habitat [HAB•ih•tat]

A place where a living thing has the food, water, and shelter it needs to live. (155)

heat [HEET]

Energy that makes things warmer. Heat can be used to cook food or melt things. (440)

 I

inclined plane
[in•KLYND PLAYN]

A simple machine that makes moving or lifting things easier. (523)

inquiry skills
[IN•kwer•ee SKILZ]

A set of skills people use to find out information. (6)

investigate [in•VES•tuh•gayt]

To plan and do a test. Scientists investigate to answer a question. (30)

leaves [LEEVZ]

The parts of a plant that make food for the plant. Leaves use light, a gas in air, and water to make food. (121)

lever [LEV•er]

A simple machine made up of a bar that pivots, or turns, on a fixed point. (523)

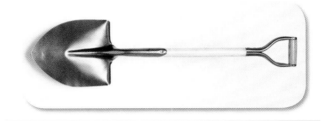

life cycle [LYF SY•kuhl]

All the stages of a plant's or an animal's life. (104, 136)

light [LYT]

A form of energy that lets you see. The sun and fire give off light energy. (441)

liquid [LIK•wid]

A form of matter that takes the shape of its container. (382)

living [LIV•ing]

Alive. Plants and animals are living things because they need food, water, and oxygen. (54)

loudness [LOWD•nuhs]

How loud or soft a sound is. (496)

 M

magnet [MAG•nit]

An object that can push and pull other magnets and pull things made of iron and steel. (530)

mammal [MAM•uhl]

The group of animals with hair or fur on their bodies. (84)

mass [MAS]

The amount of matter in an object. Mass can be measured by using a tool called a balance. (364)

matter [MAT•er]

The material all things are made of. Matter can be a solid, a liquid, or a gas. (362)

milliliter [MIL•ih•leet•er]

A unit used to measure the volume of a liquid. Milliliters are marked on many measuring cups. (384)

mineral [MIN•er•uhl]

Solid matter found in nature that was never living. Rocks are usually made of many different minerals. (211)

mixture [MIKS•cher]

A mix of different kinds of matter. Substances in a mixture do not become other substances. (404)

moon [MOON]

A huge ball of rock that orbits Earth. The moon takes almost one month to go all the way around Earth. (328)

motion [MOH•shuhn]

Movement. When something moves, it is in motion. (510)

N

natural resource
[NACH•er•uhl REE•sawrs]
Anything in nature people can use to meet their needs. (236)

nonliving [nahn•LIV•ing]
Not alive. Air, water, and rocks are nonliving. (56)

nutrients [NOO•tree•uhnts]
Substances that plants and animals need to survive. Animals get nutrients from food. Plants get nutrients from the soil. (70)

O

ocean [OH•shuhn]
A large body of salt water. Jellyfish and sharks live in oceans. (168)

orbit [AWR•bit]
The path a planet takes as it moves around the sun. Earth's orbit around the sun takes one year. (313)

oxygen [AHK•suh•juhn]
A gas in the air and water. Most living things need oxygen. (54)

pitch [PICH]

How high or low a sound is. (498)

planet [PLAN•it]

A large ball of rock or gas that moves around the sun. Earth is our planet. (312)

pole [POHL]

An end of a magnet. All magnets have a north-seeking pole and a south-seeking pole. (531)

pollution [puh•LOO•shuhn]

Waste that harms the air, water, or land. (248)

pond [PAHND]

A small, freshwater environment. Beavers and water lilies may live in a pond. (170)

precipitation [prih•sip•uh•TAY•shuhn]

Water that falls from the sky. Rain, snow, sleet, and hail are kinds of precipitation. (290)

property [PRAH•per•tee]

One part of what something is like. Color, size, and shape are each a property. (364)

R

rain forest [RAYN FAWR•ist]

An environment, with many tall trees, that gets rain almost every day. (165)

recycle [ree•SY•kuhl]

To use the materials in old things to make new things. (258)

reduce [ree•DOOS]

To use less of a resource. (258)

reflect [rih•FLEKT]

To bounce off. Light reflects when it hits most objects. (453)

repel [rih•PEL]

To push away. Poles that are the same on two magnets repel each other. (531)

reptile [REP•tyl]

The group of animals with dry skin covered in scales. (94)

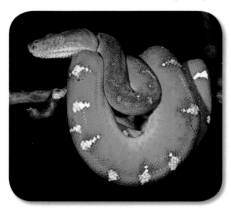

resource [REE•sawrs]

Anything people can use to meet their needs. (236)

reuse [ree•YOOZ]

To use a resource again. (258)

roots [ROOTS]

The parts of a plant that take in water and nutrients. Most roots grow underground and help hold the plant in place. (120)

rotate [ROH•tayt]

To spin around like a top. Earth rotates one time every 24 hours. (320)

S

science tools [SY•uhns TOOLZ]

Tools people use to find information. (18)

season [SEE•zuhn]

A time of year that has a certain kind of weather. The four seasons are spring, summer, fall, and winter. (277, 339)

shelter [SHEL•ter]

A safe place to live. Birds may use a nest for shelter. (63)

shrub [SHRUHB]

A bush. Shrubs have many woody stems. (129)

soil [SOYL]

Bits of rocks mixed with matter that was once living. (212)

solar energy
[SOH•ler EN•er•jee]

Energy from the sun. (442)

solar system
[SOH•ler SIS•tuhm]

The sun, its planets, and other objects that move around the sun. (312)

solid [SAHL•id]

The only form of matter that has its own shape. (372)

sound [SOWND]

Energy you can hear. Sounds are made when an object vibrates. (441, 478)

sound wave [SOWND WAYV]

Vibrations moving through matter. When sound waves reach your ears, you can hear sound. (486)

speed [SPEED]

How fast something moves. (512)

star [STAR]

A big ball of hot gas that gives off light and heat energy. The sun is the closest star to Earth. (314)

stems [STEMZ]

The parts of a plant that carry water and nutrients from the roots to the leaves. (120)

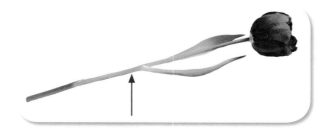

survive [ser•VYV]

To stay alive. Plants and animals need water to survive. (62)

tadpole [TAD•pohl]

A young frog. Tadpoles hatch from eggs and use gills to get oxygen from water. (106)

temperature [TEM•per•uh•cher]

A measure of how hot or cold something is. (287, 466)

texture [TEKS•cher]

The way something feels when you touch it. (373)

thermometer [ther•MAHM•uht•ter]

A tool that measures an object's temperature. (287, 466)

trunk [TRUHNK]

The one main stem of a tree. (129)

tundra [TUHN•druh]

An environment that is cold and snowy. Plants that live in a tundra are short. The animals have thick fur that helps them stay warm. (167)

vibrate [VY•brayt]

To move back and forth quickly. (478)

volcano [vahl•KAY•noh]

A place where hot melted rock called lava comes out of the ground onto Earth's surface. (203)

volume [VAHL•yoom]

The amount of space something takes up. (384)

water cycle
[WAW•ter SY•kuhl]

The movement of water from Earth's surface into the air and back to Earth's surface. (296)

water vapor
[WAWT•er VAY•per]

Water in the form of a gas. (417)

weather [WEH•ther]

What the air outside is like. The weather in summer is often sunny and hot. (276)

weather pattern

[WEH•ther PAT•ern]

A change in the weather that repeats. (276)

weathering [WEH•ther•ing]

A kind of change that happens when wind and water break down rock into smaller pieces. (200)

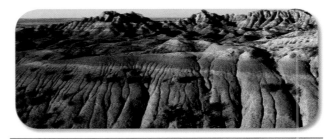

wind [WIND]

Air that is moving. (288)

Index

Gases, 260, 363, 392
  indicating magma, 348–349
  measuring, 389
  in mixtures, 394
  oxygen, 54
  sound travel through, 486–487
  water vapor, 417
Gasoline, 443
Geology, 226
Gills, 64, 96, 97, 157
Granite, 211
Grape vines, 116
Grasslands, 166
Gravity, 520
Growth
  of plants, 72
  what plants need for, 69
Guitar strings, 492

H

Habitats, 155
Hail, 290
Hair
  comparing feathers and, 83
  on manatees, 85

Hand lenses, 18, 376
Hawai'i, 180
Hearing, 480, 486
Heat, 460
  absorbed by colors, 456, 459
  from burning, 460–461
  from electricity, 462–463, 467
  as energy, 440–441
  in hot-air balloons, 429
  measuring, 466 (See also Temperature)
  movement of, 464–465
Height, measuring, 20, 375
Herons, 86
Hot-air balloons, 428–429
Howard, Ayanna, 395
Humpback whales, 489
Humus, 212, 213
Hypothesizing
  how magnets work, 529
  as inquiry skill, 8

  in investigating, 30, 32
  why sounds are different, 495

Ice, 358
  freezing, 414
  melting, 416
Iguazú Falls, South America, 378
Inches, 375
Inclined plane, 523
Inferring
  colors of butterflies, 163
  gas measurements, 389
  as inquiry skill, 8
  light from stars, 311
  liquid measurements, 381
  water in air, 295
Inner ear, 480
Inquiry skills, 6–11
  classifying, 6
  communicating, 10
  comparing, 6
  drawing conclusions, 8

R36

DIET In the wild, rainbow lorikeets eat some seeds, but their beaks aren't strong enough to eat most nuts.

CHARACTERISTIC The lorikeet's bill turns red as it gets older.

CAMOUFLAGE The rainbow lorikeet's bright colors help to hide it from predators.

HABITAT Rainbow lorikeets build their nests in hollow limbs or hollow tree trunks.